Thomas Merton

Thomas Merton

In My Own Words

The Merton Institute for Contemplative Living

Selected and Edited by Jonathan Montaldo

Liguori

LIGUORI, MISSOURI

Imprimi Potest:
Thomas D. Picton, C.Ss.R.
Provincial, Denver Province
The Redemptorists

Published by Liguori
Liguori, Missouri
www.liguori.org

Selected and Edited by Jonathan Montaldo

Library of Congress Cataloging-in-Publication Data

2007934357

ISBN 978-0-7648-1671-0

Liguori Publications, a nonprofit corporation, is an apostolate of
the Redemptorists. To learn more about the Redemptorists, visit
Redemptorists.com.

Printed in the United States of America
11 10 09 08 07   5 4 3 2 1
First edition

CONTENTS

$\mathcal{P}$REFACE

*I have never had the slightest desire to be
anything but a monk, since I came here.*

Thomas Merton was a thoroughly catholic contemplative theologian who through prayer and art discerned the presence of God incarnated into and aligned with the history of his and everyone else's life experiences. He responded to the gift of his existence with a poet's enthusiasm for the Triune God as its source. He achieved a level of sanctity, although mitigated by his limitations and human weaknesses, that mentors those who, like him, desire God's presence through all their life's things.

Merton wrote prolifically and communicated in many genres the multidimensions of his life's interests. He shaped through autobiographical writing his life's literal history during the years between his birth and death (1915–1968). He ruminated on his life's symbolic meanings that might be summarized under a poet's journey toward discovering his identity as one created to love God's image in him. He taught the lessons he had learned through his life's moral imperatives by public reflection on his chosen task to convert his heart and mind to God by becoming a Cistercian monk in community at the Abbey of Our Lady of Gethsemani in Kentucky. He allowed his readers their share in his life's mystical dimensions by recording instances of his continuing dialogues with and conversion to "God the Father" from Whom—as he once noted in a conference on prayer to his Gethsemani students—he knew himself and them capable of "receiving messages from morning until night."

In each of these four dimensions of Merton's moving and having his being (the literal, the symbolic, the moral, and the mystical), he proved himself a contemplative by his listening for God's word spoken through his life's experiences of relationship. While he guided his experience by reflection on the Scriptures and traditions of the Roman Catholic Church (he was baptized at the age of twenty-three), his life's relationships became meaningful for him as equally actual revelations of the secret presence of "the Father's" will for him in Christ through the Holy Spirit. Each facet of his existence was a "word" spoken to him for his salvation. His teaching and his art were "epiphanies" of God's merciful action in the lives of everyone else. Merton's writing was thus his conscious contribution to the salvation history of his life's intimates and all his readers.

In the future Merton will be acknowledged as one of American Catholicism's great mystical theologians. Nothing human was alien to him and, by grace and a monastic practice that opened the eye of his soul, nothing human in himself or anyone else was alien to God. He wrote transparently in private journals that are extant for a twenty-nine-year period (1939–1968). He wanted these journals published, and his honesty in them ensures that he will probably never be formally declared a saint. Yet the orthodoxy of his theology and the enthusiasm of his quest for God continue to inspire "conversion" in others who are led to live more serious, God-centered lives through his catechesis so that Merton could well one day be unofficially recognized as a "Doctor" of the universal church.

Whenever did Thomas Merton not speak or write "in his own words"? His gifts as a student and a teacher included his facility in reading a variety of world literatures with sensitivity and understanding. He gave expression to his beautifully theological mind as he appropriated a wide gamut of world literature on the experience of God. His writer's "voice" was informed by a chorus of other voices that "conversed" with him through his reading, study, and prayers. Merton was able to "translate" this chorus of voices into an idiom that communicated connections among every other human being's symbolic and mystical histories.

Since Merton's death an increasing number of edited texts have appeared that present Merton's unpublished writing, including five volumes of his letters and seven volumes of his personal journals. A plethora of books continue to appear that present selections of Merton's published work thematically so as to guide readers through the large and varied corpus of his writing. These books of selected texts help concentrate for readers a dimension of Merton's thought dispersed throughout his writing and point interested readers to the full texts just as Merton wrote them. This volume is this kind of book. Here readers have a taste of texts in which Merton speaks eloquently and often passionately on what being a monk meant for him. Merton is widely appreciated for his writing on social issues. He is valued as a poet, a figurative artist, and a photographer. His reflections on meditation and contemplative living attract readers across faith traditions. This book aims to re-engage attention to that portion of Merton's writing in which he expressed his life's core task: to realize union with God by prayer and monastic contemplative living. In this book Merton appears as who he foremost always was: a dedicated, enthusiastically Christian monk.

In one of the three texts selected to allow Merton to introduce himself "in his own words" for readers of this book, he becomes categorical: "There are three gifts I have received, for which I can never be grateful enough: first, my Catholic faith; second, my monastic vocation; third for the calling to be a writer and share my beliefs with others. I have never had the slightest desire to be anything but a monk, since I first came here." This book exposes all three of his life's blessings but with an accent on Merton's living out of the roots of long monastic tradition. Merton's writing here gives substance to his own precise definition of who he was: a gratefully Catholic monastic writer.

Jonathan Montaldo

The Merton Institute
for Contemplative Living

Louisville, Kentucky

An Introduction in Thomas Merton's Own Words

First, most of the factual information you may need can be found either in the usual reference books (*Who's Who in America, Catholic Authors,* etc.) or in books of my own.

The Seven Storey Mountain and *The Sign of Jonas* are both autobiographical. More recent information may be found in the preface to *A Thomas Merton Reader* (1962). This *Reader* is probably the handiest way of getting to know what I have written and what I think. There is a Bibliography of materials by and about me, edited by Frank Dell'Isola. This however goes only up to 1956.

To give you a quick rundown on the facts of my life: born in France, 1915. I was educated at grade schools in New York, Bermuda, France. In high school and prep school in France and England. I went to college at Cambridge, England and Columbia University, N.Y. I did graduate work at Columbia. I taught at Columbia and at St. Bonaventure University. Entered the Trappist monastery of Gethsemani in 1941 and have been here since. Ordained priest in 1949. In the monastery I have been spiritual director of the monks studying for the priesthood (Master of Students) and Master of Novices, that is to say I am supposed to guide and instruct the new ones who have just entered. I have them for three years, give them classes and so on. This takes most of my time.

People are always asking if I am still here. This

is because all sorts of rumors go around to the effect that I have left. I haven't. I am still here. I have not been seen in any New York nightclubs for twenty-five years. I am not teaching at Columbia University now. Nor am I teaching at Georgetown, Purdue, Chicago, Southern Methodist, Stanford, the Sorbonne or anywhere else except Gethsemani. I am not a priest in a parish in the Bronx or even in Brooklyn. I am not traveling around Chile giving retreats to nuns, etc. If you hear anything of this sort you can assume that it is for the birds.

People often ask why I am here in the first place, and what the contemplative life means to me. It means to me the search for truth and for God. It means finding the true significance of my life, and my right place in God's creation. It means renouncing the way of life that is led in the "world" and which, to me, is a source of illusions, confusion and deceptions. However I say this only for myself, and I have no criticism of anyone who seeks truth elsewhere and by some other way of life, provided that they really seek the truth. There are all kinds of ways to God, and ours is only one of many. But it seems to be the one for me, and it is the one I have chosen and accepted as God's will. There are three gifts I have received, for which I can never be grateful enough: first, my Catholic faith; second, my monastic vocation; third, for the calling to be a writer and share my beliefs with others. I have never had the slightest desire to be anything but a monk, since I first came here. But I have often thought I would like an even more solitary life than we have here in the monastery. I think solitude and silence are very important elements which are sadly neglected in the life of modern man, and if you want to find out more of what I think about this, there are books like *Thoughts in Solitude, New Seeds of Contemplation, The Wisdom of the Desert*, and parts of *Disputed Questions*. If you want to find out about the monastic life, besides *The Sign of Jonas*, you can also consult *The Silent Life, The Waters of Siloe*, and some of the pamphlets published here at the monastery, like *Monastic Peace*. I would be glad to send you one if you want, as a present.

For those who ask what I think about poetry (I write poetry), there is an essay published in my *Selected Poems* which deals with poetry and the contemplative life. At one time I thought I ought to give up writing poetry because it might not be compatible with the life of a monk, but I don't think this any more. People ask me how I write poetry. I just write it. I get an idea and I put it down, and add to it, and take away what is useless, and try to end up with some kind of poem. A poem is for me the expression of an inner poetic experience, and what matters is the experience, more than the poem itself. Some of my favorite poets are St.-John Perse (Alexis Léger), F. García

Lorca, Dylan Thomas, Gerard Manley Hopkins, Boris Pasternak, William Blake, John Donne, Dante, Shakespeare, Tu Fu, Isaias, Aeschylus, Sophocles, etc.

To those who ask what I think about art, there are a couple of essays on the subject in *Disputed Questions*. I like modern art. I have always liked such painters as Picasso, Chagall, Cézanne, Rouault, Matisse, and so on. I like expressionists and impressionists and post-impressionists and abstract expressionists and most of the other "—ists" but I don't like social realism. Nor do I like candy-box art or the illustrations in the *Saturday Evening Post*. I am not prepared to enter into an argument in defense of these preferences.

Some may want to know what I think about politics. I think that we citizens of the United States, as a nation, ought to make more serious efforts to act our age and think in proportion to our size. For this, a whole lot of people who never thought about anything serious in their lives are going to have to wake up and start thinking about their moral and political responsibilities. It is no good going on emotions and prejudices and slogans and feelings of righteous indignation. It is no good simply letting our minds become a passive reflection of a television screen. It is no good going around shouting something that someone else has suggested that we shout, no matter what it may be. If we want to become a seriously political nation, the <u>people have got to do some thinking for themselves.</u>

I think two issues in this country are extremely serious: one, <u>the race issue;</u> two, the question of <u>nuclear war.</u> The second one is worse than the first but both of them are pretty bad. I do not believe that people who fight for integration are all Communists. I do not think that people who are opposed to nuclear war are necessarily enemies of America and paid agents of Communism. I do not think that military might is the solution to our problems. It may defend our pocket books, but it will never defend our liberty. <u>Liberty begins inside our own souls.</u> Our souls cannot be free if we believe only in money and power and comfort and having a good time. I do not think that our present line of action is doing anything to keep us free.

Doubtless I could go on to explain what I think about jazz (I like it); the movies (haven't seen one for years, don't miss them); smoking (don't miss it); TV (never watched it, don't want to); the newspapers (seldom see one); modern youth (I like them, at least the kind we've got around here—they are the only ones I know); cars (I never had one, can get along without). There must be some other things about which I ought to have an opinion, but this is enough.

CIRCULAR LETTER TO FRIENDS:
TO "MY DEAR FRIEND" (CA. 1963), IN *THE ROAD TO JOY*

$\mathcal{I}$ have lately tried to avoid writing simply as a propagandist for a particular cause or for a limited program. I am not merely a spokesman for a contemplative or monastic movement, and I am not purely and simply a "spiritual writer."

The earliest pieces of writing in this book [A Thomas Merton Reader] are two book reviews done for the New York Herald Tribune Books in May of 1938. These were written when I was a graduate student at Columbia, about six months before my baptism into the Catholic Church. About three years later I entered the novitiate of the Cistercian Abbey of Gethsemani to become what is popularly called a "Trappist" monk. There are a few poems written when I was living in Greenwich Village and later when I was teaching English at St. Bonaventure College [in Olean, New York]. But the vast majority of these pages were written at Gethsemani, and of these a very fair proportion represents work done in the last six years.

I would say that my life at Gethsemani has fallen roughly into four periods. First, the novitiate. I was a novice in 1942–1944. Those were hard years, before the days when radiators were much in favor during the winter, when the hours of communal prayer were much longer, when the fasts were much stricter. It was a period of training, and a happy, austere one, during which I wrote little. The best Gethsemani poems belong to this period.

At the end of the novitiate my health broke down and I was appointed to write and do translations of French books and articles. I was also studying philosophy and theology in preparation for ordination to the priesthood. This second period extends from 1944, my first vows, to ordination in 1949. At first the writing done was very bad. Two books were written which are *not* represented here, although they were unfortunately published [*Exile Ends in Glory* (1948) and *What Are These Wounds* (1950)]. In 1946 I wrote *The Seven Storey Mountain*, in 1947 *Seeds of Contemplation*, and in 1948 *The Waters of Siloe*. After ordination, in 1949, there was another brief period of poor health and nervous exhaustion. I was almost incapable of writing for at least a year and a half after I became a priest. Then after a rest period in the hospital, I wrote *The Ascent to Truth* and *Bread in the Wilderness* (both about 1951) and finished *The Sign of Jonas*, 1952. In 1951 I was appointed the Master of the Scholastics, that is, of the young monks studying for ordination in the monastery. This entailed a fair amount of work preparing conferences and classes. Books like *The Living Bread* and particularly *No Man Is an Island* and *The Silent Life* belong to the end of this period.

Finally a fourth stage In 1955 I was made Master of the Choir Novices. This is an office involving a considerable amount of work and responsibility. No writing of any account was done in 1956, but after that it was possible to produce short books or collections of essays, and some poetry. *Disputed Questions, The Wisdom of the Desert, The Behavior of Titans*, and *New Seeds of Contemplation* belong to this last period. So too do more recent essays on nuclear war, on Chinese thought, on liturgy, and on solitude.

The books of the second period are the ones most widely known and read. The books and articles of the fourth period are, perhaps naturally, the ones that seem most significant to me. Maybe one reason for this is that, to me at least, they represent a successful attempt to escape the limitations that I inevitably created for myself with *The Seven Storey Mountain*, a refusal to be content with the artificial public image which this autobiography created.

A THOMAS MERTON READER

You ask for some information about our life here... This monastery is a contemplative community, that is to say we are monks who live strictly within our monastery and do not go outside into the world except for very exceptional reasons. We keep a strict rule of silence, not speaking to one another except when it is essential. Our life is devoted to prayer, and we live under a relatively strict discipline of poverty and obedience. Of course, like all Christian monks, we are obliged to chastity. I say our poverty is relatively strict: we possess nothing at all, but the standard of life in the monastery would not appear poor to a resident in Pakistan, though it is relatively poor in America. That is to say we lack many of the comforts and conveniences that American people regard as necessities, and we live by our manual labor and the produce of our farm. Our clothing is poor and simple, and our food also. The diet is vegetarian.

As a community, the monastery is chiefly cenobitic [monks who live in community] in its spirit. Emphasis is on the choral prayer, which consists mainly of recitation of psalms. We rise at two o'clock in the morning and chant the night vigils until about four. Then we have other prayers or readings and meditations, alternating with work and study throughout the day until evening when we retire at seven.

Some of us in the community, and I am one of these, have aspirations for a more solitary and meditative form of prayer life. Our situation is a little difficult, but it is possible to obtain permission for a certain latitude in this respect. Thus I am allowed by the Father Abbot to spend a certain part of the day, often an entire afternoon, in a little house in the woods where there is complete silence and isolation, and it is possible to give oneself completely to meditative prayer. I feel that in some respects our situation is a little analogous to that of the Sufis in their relation with the orthodox Moslem community with its emphasis on legal observance.

You ask about Our Lady of Gethsemani: the monasteries of our Order are dedicated to Mary. The meaning of this dedication may be understood in different manners by different types of monks. For my part, I consider that each monastery dwells so to speak surrounded and protected by the maternal love of Mary, and by her prayers in heaven. If we are dedicated to the mystery of Gethsemani, it means to say that we are in particular to be mindful of the Blessed Virgin's solitude and sorrow of heart in her compassion for the suffering of Christ in the Garden of Gethsemani where He was abandoned by all who loved Him and was betrayed by one of His disciples. I think then that this means our life as monks is lived especially under the sign of a kind of inner solitude and dereliction, and I know from experience that this is true. But in this solitude and dereliction we are united with others who are alone and solitary and poor.

LETTER TO ABDUL AZIZ, JANUARY 30, 1961, IN *THE HIDDEN GROUND OF LOVE*

ON THE ROAD TO
BECOMING A MONK

Christ, from my cradle, I had known You everywhere,
And even though I sinned, I walked in You, and knew
You were my world:
You were my France and England,
My seas and my America:
You were my life and air,
and yet I would not own You....

I trace my days back to another childhood,
Exchanging, as I go,
New York and Cuba for Your Galilee,
And Cambridge for Your Nazareth,
Until I come again to my beginning,
And find a manger, star and straw,
A pair of animals, some simple men.
And thus I learn that I was born,
Now not in France, but Bethlehem.

FROM "THE BIOGRAPHY,"
IN COLLECTED POEMS

Toward the Only Real City in America

𝓜other wanted me to be independent, and not to run with the herd. I was to be original, individual, I was to have a definite character and ideals of my own. I was not to be an article thrown together, on the common bourgeois pattern, on everybody else's assembly line.

If we had continued as we had begun, and if John Paul and I had grown up in that house, probably this Victorian-Greek complex would have built itself up gradually, and we would have turned into good-mannered and earnest skeptics, polite, intelligent, and perhaps even in some sense useful. We might have become successful authors, or editors of magazines, professors at small and progressive colleges. The way would have been all smooth and perhaps I would never have ended up as a monk.

But it is not yet the time to talk about that happy consummation, the thing for which I most thank and praise God, and which is of all things the ultimate paradoxical fulfillment of my mother's ideals for me—the last thing she would ever have dreamed of: the boomerang of all her solicitude for an individual development.

THE SEVEN STOREY MOUNTAIN

$\mathcal{P}$op had sent us [Merton was living with his father Owen in France] money at Christmas, and we used some of it to buy a big expensive three-volume set of books, full of pictures, called *Le Pays de France*. And I shall never forget the fascination with which I studied it, and filled my mind with those cathedrals and ancient abbeys and those castles and towns and monuments of the culture that had so captivated my heart.

I remember how I looked at the ruins of Jumièges and Cluny, and wondered how those immense basilicas had looked in the days of their glory. Then there was Chartres, with its two unequal spires; the long vast nave of Bourges; the soaring choir of Beauvais; the strange fat Romanesque cathedral of Angoulème, and the white Byzantine domes of Pèrigueux. And I gazed upon the huddled buildings of the ancient Grande Chartreuse, crowded together in their solitary valley, with the high mountains loaded with firs, soaring up to their rocky summits on either side. What kind of men had lived in those cells? I cannot say that I wondered much about that, as I looked at the pictures. I had no curiosity about monastic vocations or religious rules, but I know my heart was filled with a kind of longing to breathe the air of that lonely valley and to listen to its silence. I wanted to be in all these places, which the pictures of *Le Pays de France* showed me: indeed, it was a kind of problem to me and an unconscious source of obscure and half-realized woe that I could not be in all of them at once.

THE SEVEN STOREY MOUNTAIN

I had been in Rome before, on an Easter vacation from school, for about a week. I had seen the Forum and the Coliseum and the Vatican museum and St. Peter's. But I had not really seen Rome....

I never knew what relics and what wonderful and holy things were hidden in the churches whose doors and aisles and arches had become the refuge of my mind. Christ's cradle and the pillar of the Flagellation and the True Cross and St. Peter's chain, and the tombs of the great martyr St. Cecilia and of Pope St. Clement and of the great deacon St. Lawrence who was burned on a gridiron.…These things did not speak to me, or at least I did not know they spoke to me. But the churches that enshrined them did, and so did the art on their walls.

And now for the first time in my life I began to find out something of Who this Person was that men called Christ.…

The saints of those forgotten days had left upon the walls of their churches the words which by the peculiar grace of God I was able in some measure to apprehend, although I could not decode them all. But above all, the realest and most immediate source of this grace was Christ Himself, present in those churches, in all His power, and in His Humanity, in His Human Flesh and His material, physical, corporeal Presence. How often I was left entirely alone in these churches with this tremendous God, and knew nothing of it—except I had to know something of it, as I say, obscurely. And it was He who was teaching me Who He was, more directly than I was capable of realizing.

THE SEVEN STOREY MOUNTAIN

Such was the death of the hero, the great man I had wanted to be. Externally (I thought) I was a big success. Everybody knew who I was at Columbia. Those who had not found out, soon did when the Yearbook came out, full of pictures of myself. It was enough to tell them more about me than I intended, I suppose. They did not have to be very astute to see through the dumb self-satisfied expression in all those portraits. The only thing that surprises me is that no one openly reproached or mocked me for such ignominious vanity. No one threw eggs at me, nobody said a word. And yet I know how capable they were of saying many words, not tastefully chosen, perhaps, but deadly enough.

If my nature had been more stubborn in clinging to the pleasures that disgusted me: if I had refused to admit that I was beaten by this futile search for satisfaction where it could not be found, if my moral and nervous constitution had not caved in under the weight of my own emptiness, who can tell what would eventually have happened to me? Who could tell where I would have ended?

I had come very far, to find myself in this blind alley: but the very anguish and helplessness of my position was something to which I rapidly succumbed. And it was my defeat that was to be the occasion of my rescue.

THE SEVEN STOREY MOUNTAIN

Some kind of instinct prompted me to go to Sixteenth Street to the Jesuit Church of St. Francis Xavier. I had never been there. I don't know what I was looking for....

It was some kind of novena service, maybe a Holy Hour, I don't know: but it was nearly ending. Just as I found a place and fell on my knees, they began singing the *Tantum Ergo*....All these people, workmen, poor women, students, clerks, singing the Latin Hymn to the Blessed Sacrament written by St. Thomas Aquinas.

I fixed my eyes on the monstrance, on the white Host.

And then it suddenly became clear to me that my whole life was at a crisis. Far more than I could imagine or understand or conceive was now hanging upon a word—a decision of mine.

I had not shaped my life to this situation: I had not been building up to this. Nothing had been further from my mind. There was, therefore, an added solemnity in the fact that I had been called in here abruptly to answer a question that had been preparing, not in my mind, but in the infinite depths of an eternal Providence.

I did not clearly see it then, but I think now that it might have been something in the nature of a last chance. If I had hesitated or refused at that moment—what would have become of me?

But the way into the new land, the promised land, the land that was not like the Egypt where I persisted in living, was now thrown open again: and I instinctively sensed that it was only for a moment.

It was a moment of crisis, yet of interrogation: a moment of searching, but it was a moment of joy. It took me about a minute to collect my thoughts about the grace that had been suddenly implanted in my soul, and to adjust the weak eyes of my spirit to its unaccustomed light, and during that moment my whole life remained suspended on the edge of an abyss: but this time, the abyss was an abyss of love and peace, the abyss was God.

It would be in some sense a blind, irrevocable act to throw myself over. But if I failed to do that…I did not even have to turn and look behind me at what I would be leaving. Wasn't I tired enough of all that?

So now the question faced me:

"Do you really want to be a priest? If you do, say so…"

The hymn was ending. The priest collected the ends of the humeral veil over his hands that held the base of the monstrance, and slowly lifted it off the altar, and turned to bless the people.

I looked straight at the Host, and I knew, now, Who it was that I was looking at, and I said:

"Yes, I want to be a priest, with all my heart I

want it. If it is Your will, make me a priest—make me a priest."

When I had said them, I realized in some measure what I had done with those last four words, what power I had put into motion on my behalf, and what a union had been sealed between me and that power by my decision.

THE SEVEN STOREY MOUNTAIN

Snow comes early at St. Bonaventure's, and when the snow came, I used to say the Little Hours of the Breviary walking in the deep untrodden drifts along the wood's edge, towards the river. No one would ever come and disturb me out there in all that silence, under the trees, which made a noiseless, rudimentary church over my head, between me and the sky. It was wonderful out there when the days were bright, even though the cold bit down into the roots of my fingernails as I held the open Breviary in my hands. I could look up from the book, and recite the parts I already knew by heart, gazing at the glittering, snow-covered hills, white and gold and planted with bare woods, standing out bright against the blinding blue sky. Oh, America, how I began to love your country! What miles of silences God has made in you for contemplation! If only people realized what all your mountains and forests are really for!

The new year came, 1941. In its January, I was

1941

to have my twenty-sixth birthday, and enter upon my twenty-seventh, most momentous year.

Already, in February, or before that, the idea came to me that I might make a retreat in some monastery for Holy Week and Easter. Where would it be? The first place that came into my mind was the Trappist abbey Dan Walsh had told me about, in Kentucky. As soon as I thought about it, I saw that this was the only choice. That was where I needed to go. Something had opened out, inside me, in the last months, something that required, demanded at least a week in that silence, in that austerity, praying together with the monks in their cold choir.

And my heart expanded with anticipation and happiness.

THE SEVEN STOREY MOUNTAIN

We began to climb the wide stairs. Our steps echoed in the empty darkness. One flight and then another and a third and a fourth. There was an immense distance between floors; it was a building with great high ceilings. Finally we came to the top floor, and the Brother opened the door into a wide room, and put down my bag, and left me.

I heard his steps crossing the yard below, to the gate house.

And I felt the deep, deep silence of the night, and of peace, and of holiness enfold me like love, like safety.

The embrace of it, the silence! I had entered into a solitude that was an impregnable fortress. And the silence enfolded me, spoke to me, and spoke louder and more eloquently than any voice, and in the middle of that quiet, sweet-smelling room with the moon pouring its peacefulness in through the open window, with the warm night air, I realized truly whose house that was, O glorious Mother of God!…

How shall I be able to explain or communicate to those who have not seen these holy houses, your consecrated churches and Cistercian cloisters, the might of the truths that overpowered me all the days of that week?

Yet no one will find it hard to conceive the impression made on a man thrown suddenly into a Trappist monastery at four o'clock in the morning, after the night office, as I was the following day.…

The cloister was cold, and dimly lit, and the smell of damp wool astounded me by its unearthliness. And I saw the monks. There was one, right there, by the door, he had knelt, or rather thrown himself down before a *pietà* in the cloister corner, and had buried his head in the huge sleeves of his cowl there at the feet of the dead Christ, the Christ Who lay in the arms of Mary, letting fall one arm and a pierced hand in the limpness of death. It was a picture so fierce that it scared me: the abjection, the dereliction of this seemingly shattered monk at the feet of the broken Christ. I stepped into the cloister as if into an abyss....

And now the church was full of light, and the monks stood in their stalls and bowed like white seas at the end of the psalms, those slow, rich, somber and yet lucid tones of the psalms, praising God in His new morning, thanking Him for the world He had created and for the life He continued to give it....

The eloquence of this liturgy was even more tremendous: and what it said was one, simple, cogent, tremendous truth: this church, the court of the Queen of Heaven, is the real capital of the country in which we are living. This is the center of all the vitality that is in America. This is the cause and reason why the nation is holding together. These men, hidden in the anonymity of their choir and their white cowls, are doing for their land what no army, no congress, no president could ever do as such: they are winning for it the grace and protection and the friendship of God.

THE SEVEN STOREY MOUNTAIN

St. Bonventure, New York
December 6, 1941

Finally has come the time to go to the Trappists
and try to get in.

I cannot explain this except to say it in a lot of
different ways: time to get out of the subway and go
to the clean woods; or time to get out of the party
full of smoke and pray in a clean bedroom, like
before sleeping and resting the way it is sweet. It is
time to stop arguing with the seven guys who argue
inside my head and be completely quiet in front of
the face of Peace.

It is time for the midnight to get very quiet
(through me giving to somebody else everything I
am thought to be) so that my house may be at rest,
and the soul talk in peace and listen to Peace and
learn from Peace.…

No, honestly: it is time to stop being sick,
(better than before, of course) and really get well.
It is time to be full of peace and silence. And if
you have a free and real choice between a world
that belongs in a book by John O'Hara and one
that belongs in a book by St. Theresa of Ávila, I
guess you have to make the choice in order to be
happy, and quit arguing as if the two were even
comparable.

Once I can be in the place where I belong
entirely to God and not to anyone less than Him,

like some writer having my legal name, then I guess problems about writing and everything else will not be much problems any more. Harlem isn't it, for me. Nor is any college. Nor is New York.

Maybe St. Lucy's Day I start out for Kentucky, full of prayer. (Next Saturday). And round His sunny tent like lambs rejoice. Also, there is absolutely no language to say the things there are to say, about this, except the language of love: but there He will teach me to use that language like a child and a saint. Until which, I cannot talk about Him, Who is all I want to talk about.

And in Him while I sing in the big church, (I pray on my face He will let me!) in Him will be also: Lax, Gibney, Seymour, Slate, Rice, Gerdy, Knight, Huttlinger; and Van Doren, and the Baroness, and Mary Jerdo and my brother and my uncle and aunt and my father and mother who died and Bramachari and the whole mystical body of Christ, everybody, Roger, Gil, all people, Jinny, Lilly, All. All people. The living and the dead. All days, all times, all ages, all worlds, all mysteries, all miracles…

LETTER TO BOB LAX, IN *THE ROAD TO JOY*

The life of each one in this abbey is part of a mystery. We all add up to something far beyond ourselves. We cannot yet realize what it is. But we know, in the language of our theology, that we are all members of the Mystical Christ, and that we all grow together in Him for Whom all things are created.

In one sense we are always traveling, and traveling as if we did not know where we were going.

In another sense we have already arrived.

We cannot arrive at the perfect possession of God in this life and this is why we are traveling and in darkness. But we already possess Him by grace, and therefore in that sense we have arrived and are dwelling in the light.

But oh! How far have I to go to find You in Whom I have already arrived!

THE SEVEN STOREY MOUNTAIN

$\mathcal{L}$ady, when on that night I left the Island that was once your England, your love went with me, although I could not know it, and could not make myself aware of it. And it was your love, your intercession for me, before God, that was preparing the seas before my ship, laying open the way for me to another country.

I was not sure where I was going, and I could not see what I would do when I got to New York. But you saw further and clearer than I, and you opened the seas before my ship, whose track led me across the waters to a place I had never dreamed of, and which you were even then preparing for me to be my rescue and my shelter and my home. And when I thought there was no God and no love and no mercy, you were leading me all the while into the midst of His love and His mercy, and taking me, without my knowing anything about it, to the house that would hide me in the secret of His Face.

Glorious Mother of God, shall I ever again distrust you, or your God, before Whose throne you are irresistible in your intercession? Shall I ever turn my eyes from your hand and from your face and from your eyes? Shall I ever look anywhere else but in the face of your love, to find out true counsel, and to know my way, in all the days and all the moments of my life?

As you have dealt with me, Lady, deal with all my millions of brothers who live in the same misery that I knew then: lead them in spite of themselves and guide them by your tremendous influence, O Holy Queen of souls and refuge of sinners, and bring them to your Christ the way you brought me. *Illos tuos misericordes oculos ad nos converte, et Jesum, benedictum fructum ventris tui, nobis ostende.* Show us your Christ, Lady, after this our exile, yes: but show Him to us also now, show Him to us here, while we are still wanderers.

THE SEVEN STOREY MOUNTAIN

Coming to the monastery has been for me exactly the right kind of withdrawal. It has given me perspective. It has taught me how to live. And now I owe everyone else in the world a share in that life. My first duty is to start, for the first time, to live as a member of a human race which is no more (and no less) ridiculous than I am myself. And my first human act is the recognition of how much I owe everybody else.

Thus God has brought me to Kentucky where the people are, for the most part, singularly without inhibitions. This is the precise place God has chosen for my sanctification. Here I must revise all my own absurd plans, and take myself as I am, Gethsemani as it is, and America as it is—atomic bomb and all. It is utterly peculiar, but nonetheless true that, after all, one's nationality should come to have a meaning in the light of eternity. I have lived for thirty-six years without one. Nine years ago I was proud of the fact. I thought that to be a citizen of heaven all you had to do was throw away your earthly passport. But now I have discovered a mystery: that Miss Sue and all the other ladies in the office of the Deputy Clerk of the Louisville District Court are perhaps in some accidental way empowered to see that I am definitely admitted to the Kingdom of Heaven forever.

THE SIGN OF JONAS

His Life at Gethsemani Excerpted in Letters to His Teacher at Columbia, Mark Van Doren

April 14, 1942

We are allowed to write letters very seldom, but I got special permission to send you some of my poems. I have been writing here. Also, I enclose a page or two of a Journal I have been keeping: it is completely to do with religious experience—& so are the poems, & so is my life, naturally.

And what a life! It is tremendous. Not because of any acts we perform, any penance, any single feature of the liturgy or the chant, not because we sleep on boards & straw mattresses & fast & work & sweat & sing & keep silence. These things are all utterly simple acts that have no importance whatever in themselves. But the whole unity of the life is tremendous. That is because the life *is* a real unity, because the foundation of its unity is God's unity: the ontological basis of our life is the simplicity & the purity of God. His simplicity *is* our life. We *live* His oneness: we *live* His singleness of concentration on His own immense purity and goodness. No wonder it is wonderful. The life is God: it is Christ, in the sense that Christ is the principle & end of absolutely everything that a

Trappist does, right down to breathing. Really, I have only one reason for living at all and that is the love, the glory, the good pleasure of Christ. Therefore, since this is the sort of thing men were created to do (not necessarily all as Trappists, of course) I am very happy. I never was really unhappy in my life except perhaps for a while when I was most mixed up—the year I was registered at Columbia but hardly ever came to school, although I was supposed to be doing everything there was to do on campus beside classes too.

Now I am here, it already seems quite clear how the whole of my life until I came here is at last intelligible. All that chaos, France & England & everywhere else I lived, straightens itself out & points to our cloisters & our fields...

THE ROAD TO JOY

April 16, 1944

Day by day in this monastery I realize more & more how far I have failed to show gratitude to all the people who have been kind to me—& realize also how inadequate my thanks really are! Not the least of these good friends is yourself. A series of cryptic messages from [Bob] Lax tells me that [James] Laughlin has taken the poems and is printing them. So I thank you—and the poems thank you. And if my thanks are, as they are, far short of adequate, let me add that Jesus said that

anyone who gave a cup of cold water to one of
His little ones would not be without his reward.
And that you have done this good thing for the
poems—which are Christ's poems and not mine,
insofar as there is any good in them—you have
begun to have your reward. "Love is repaid by love
alone" says St. John of the Cross. So what can I
give you by way of thanks? I offer you your own
charity, which is in you from Christ, through the
Holy Spirit—and which is, insofar as it is of & from
Him—my charity also & everybody's charity, & is
the same infinite & simple & eternal act of Love,
in Whom we are all one, uttering Himself in one
of His multitudinous utterances in time. For every
good work we do speaks the Name of Christ, in
Whom is all Truth, Love & Reality, & Who is the
actuality of everything that is…

 I can bless you now as a monk, for I have made
profession, & my novitiate is over, I am a Cistercian
monk, I have a cowl. This cowl—I wear it, or rather
I dwell in it. It is the most beautiful of garments.
It is like the cloud that protected the children of
Israel in the desert. It is as voluminous as a house.
It hides & embraces my mortality like the Immortal
Soul of Christ, & is the symbol of His humanity, in
which I live, & for which I live: which is also, the
"Whole Christ—the Head & the Members"—the
Church.

 If I could only say how dead I was and how

alive I am. Only our Easter liturgy can say it for me. Someday I hope you will come & visit us. Our house is full of love & peace…

THE ROAD TO JOY

November 4, 1947

It is such a long time since I wrote to you that I am in another age of the monastic life and definitely feel it, too. I made my solemn vows last March (and re-make them in my heart every day!) and I am going on towards the priesthood which is about two years away. When I say I feel it—I mean this. I can see all the big responsibilities beginning to creep up on me: material offices and cares, jobs in the community, etc. Just where I least expected it I can see that I will have to confront the problem of not becoming that middle-aged professional man whose shadow I thought I was escaping.

I am tremendously busy with writing.…

What grows on me most is the desire for solitude—to vanish completely and go off into some desert and never be heard of again—& pray, & keep still. Sometimes this desire is a temptation (whenever it takes some concrete form and presents itself with a map of Arizona in its hand) but otherwise it is a grace—and all I know about it is that I must have it undefined for the moment & that God will make the details and circumstances of it take shape in His own

good time: and it probably won't be a desert but
something better....

THE ROAD TO JOY

March 30, 1948

I can no longer see the ultimate meaning of a man's
life in terms of either "being a poet" or "being a
contemplative" or even in a certain sense in "being
a saint" (although that is the only thing to be). It
must be something much more immediate than
that. I—and every other person in the world—*must*
say: "I have my own special, peculiar destiny which
no one else ever has had or ever will have. There
exists for me a particular goal, a fulfillment which
must be all my own—nobody else's—& it does not
really identify that destiny to put it under some
category—"poet," "monk," "hermit." Because my
own individual destiny is a meeting, an encounter
with God that he has destined for me alone. His
glory in me will be to receive from me something
He can never receive from anyone else—because
it is a gift of His to me which He has never given
to anyone else & never will. My whole life is only
that—to establish that particular constant with
God which is the one He has planned for my
eternity!"

Once that contact is established—I feel it in
my bones & it sets me on fire—the possibilities
are *without end.* Unlimited fruitfulness, life,

productivity, vision, peace. Yet I have no way of saying just what it will be. I don't think it will be merely writing & I don't think it will be anything I have ever yet known as contemplation & in fact I don't think it will be anything that anyone on earth can see or understand—especially myself.

In the light of all that it doesn't make so much sense any more to be planning to either renounce or to adopt whole "blocks" of activity—cutting out "all" writing or "going into solitude for good" (as I would like to)—the thing is to take a new line & let everything be determined by immediate circumstances that manifest God's will & His action here & now. No matter where it may lead, because I don't really know anyway & I don't have to know provided that God is doing the leading....

THE ROAD TO JOY

April 8, 1949

Tomorrow is Palm Sunday. I am a deacon now and that gives me some special things to sing in the Easter Liturgy—a closer participation, materially and spiritually, in everything that is going on. It really does have a considerable effect on a person to take part in these things. I know the priesthood is going to be something tremendous. A kind of death, to begin with. But that is good. The whole business about Orders has been striking me as something much more important than religious vows. The question of sacramental character comes in, for one thing. Then you become public property. At the same time you are mystically more isolated in God. The combination is quite baffling.

Anyway the priesthood will end up giving me a completely social function. Perhaps that was what I was always trying to escape. Actually, having run into it at this end of the circle, it is making me what I was meant to be and I am about to exist.

As soon as I put on the vestments of a subdeacon and stood in the sanctuary I was bowled over by the awareness that this was what I was always supposed to wear, and everything else, so far, had been something of a disguise.

THE ROAD TO JOY

December 30, 1955

Your wonderful letter from Beaune [Côte d'Or, France] was a happy surprise. Thank you for thinking of me at the Grande Chartreuse. Even to be thought of there is something. Thanks for telling me about Bob [Lax], and above all thanks for the poem, which is so true to him. I even put it up in the novitiate so that all could ponder on a poem about a spiritual subject. You don't know, do you, that I am now master of the novices—a much more responsible and occupying job than the other one. I have practically a small kingdom of my own, a wing of the monastery in which Canon Law says

I am the boss. The young ones entering live there and depend on the broken reed they have received as their support. The best of it is that the place is quiet, and we have our own garden and chapel, and the job is not too plaguing. In fact I find that if I overcome a little of my selfishness, it is quite pleasant.

Imagine if you can what led up to it. Again the old wrestling, more awful than before, about solitude. This last year I really plunged into the fight for true. I found a couple of people who told me "Yes, you should leave, you should go off and live alone—or enter another order etc., etc." Armed with this I even got as far as Rome (I mean with pestering letters) and finally the highest Superiors under the Pope calmed me down and told me to stay here. It sounds silly but I had to go through it. Having done so I feel pretty well cleaned out. I mean washed of everything. There is very little I seem to want at all—or so it seems, until I turn around and realize that I still cling to this bodily life, for instance. It would be too impossible of me if I suddenly turned out to be detached from that. Actually, I think the only valid step that has come out of the whole thing is that I am now detached from detachment. And from ideals, I no longer want to know, or to think, what I am or what I've got or where I'm going...

THE ROAD TO JOY

February 11, 1956

For the rest I lecture the novices on Cassian and
on the customs of the twelfth-century monks and
on the behavior of twentieth-century novices and
secretly I pry into the psychoanalysts. These are the
occupations which God has given to the Master
of Novices in Cistercian monasteries. I have no
other, except the felling of trees, and the praying
of prayers. In the distance, on top of the hill, I can
see the fire tower when I look out the windows of
the novitiate. In the evening it is surrounded with
seraphim.

Come to Kentucky some more.

THE ROAD TO JOY

February 24, 1966

There is no need to tell you where I am. You have
seen the hermitage and I am living in it—have
been really for over a year, but only in the last six
months have I been free of any job or obligation
in the monastery, so I am here all the time. I just
go down to the monastery once a day for Mass and
a cooked meal. It is a serious, by no means idyllic
sort of life—quite a lot of cold here in January
and February, and one takes stock of, gets to grips
with, a lot of things. What infinite nonsense is in
the world and it turns out I am not exempt from
much of it: I have to sweat it out of myself here.

In a way the best thing about the life is chopping
wood. And then burning it in a good lively fire, and
making tea, and reading St. Thomas or the Desert
Fathers or the Bible or more recently the tales
about a mad Persian called Nasrudin, who seems
to have been the subject of all the good jokes that
ever go into anything later, from Don Quixote to
the Marx Bros....

THE ROAD TO JOY

July 23, 1968

And then, man, I fly to Asia. Really, that is the
plan. All sorts of places I am supposed to go to if I
don't faint from delight at the mere thought. Since
I hop from Singapore to Darjeeling, and have a
meeting there with various swamis gurus etc. I
hope to sneak into Nepal. Then maybe a bit more
of the top of India. Then Thailand (if not Burma,
hard to get into, but may manage), then Indonesia
(a monastery of ours there) then Japan, then home.
Maybe. If they can get me home, I should say. This
doesn't begin until October but at the moment I
am itching with vaccinations and expectations
and being photographed for the passprops [sic] and
phonographed for the pesthouse and airlifted to
the quarantine and divided up into computers. If
I survive I may manage to get to a country where
they don't even have roads. And where if you ride
it's on an ox or not at all. Or a yak. Or an elephamp

[sic]. All this because of a meeting of dull Abbots in Thailand, but who would not go to a meeting of Abbots for all those other secondary gains?...

Right now, as I say, I am taken up with getting shots and visas, and cleaning up my premises and finishing up all the absurd jobs I took on when I was a low creature of earth and not a prospective world traveler. I assure you I hope to make the best of it while its lasts! (Think of all the cablegrams saying "RETURN AT ONCE" being shot to Bali, Tibet, Kamchatka, Ceylon, the Maldives, the Endives, the Southern Chives, the Lesser Maundies, the Nether Freeways, the Outer Salvages).

THE ROAD TO JOY

Who Is a Monk?

Teach us, Cistercian Fathers, how to wear
Silence, our humble armor.
Pray us a torrent of the seven spirits
That are our wine and stamina:
Because your work is not yet done.
But look: the valleys shine with promises,
And every burning morning is a prophecy of Christ
Coming to raise and vindicate
Even our sorry flesh.

Then will your graves, Gethsemani,
give up their angels,
Return them to their souls to learn
The songs and attitudes of glory.
Then will creation rise again like gold
Clean, from the furnace of your litanies:
The beasts and trees shall share your resurrection,
And a new world be born from these green tombs.

FROM "THE TRAPPIST CEMETARY–GETHSEMANI,"
IN COLLECTED POEMS

$\mathcal{I}$n almost all the great religions of the world we find special groups of men and women who separate themselves from the ordinary life of society, take upon themselves particular and difficult obligations, and devote themselves to one task above all: to deepening their understanding and practice of their own religion in its most basic implications.

In Hinduism, the monk seeks deliverance from

the earthly round of time and delusion by ascetic and mystical purification. In Buddhism he seeks enlightenment as to the ground of his own being. In Judaism, shortly before the time of Christ, the monks at Qumran lived in the full eschatological consciousness of Old Testament prophecy. In Islam, though the Sufis are not "monks," they have traditionally sought the deepest ecstatic experience of union with God. In Christianity the monk seeks before all else to live out his faith in and according to the gospel of Jesus Christ by renouncing himself, taking up the cross of self-denial and following Christ. He unites himself with the hidden years of labor spent by Jesus in Nazareth, or he follows Jesus into the desert sharing the Master's solitary prayer.

MONASTIC LIFE AT GETHSEMANI

The Monk and the Gospel

The Catholic monastic life is the response to Jesus Christ's call to penance and prayer in the Gospel. All Christians seek to save their souls by following Christ. Monks, however, pay strict attention to the injunctions of the Master, seek to observe more closely and more faithfully such words as the following:

"Take heed to yourselves lest your hearts be overcharged with surfeiting and drunkenness, and the cares of this life, and that (last) day come upon you suddenly…Watch therefore, praying at all times that you may be accounted worthy...to stand before the Son of Man" (Luke 21:34–36).

"If any man will come after me, let him deny himself and take up his cross, and follow me. For he that will save his life shall lose it, and he that shall lose his life for my sake shall find it. For what does it profit a man if he gain the whole world and suffer the loss of his own soul?" (Matthew 16:24–26).

"If you will be perfect, go, sell what you have and give to the poor, and you shall have treasure in heaven, and come, follow me" (Matthew 19:21).

"If any one love me, he will keep my word and my Father will love him, and we will come to him and will make our abode with him...Abide in my love. If you keep my commandments you shall abide in my love, as I have kept my Father's commandments and abide in his love (John 14:23 and 15:9–10).

"And the multitude of believers had but one heart and one soul, neither did any one say that any of the things which he had was his own: but all things were common unto them" (Acts 4:32).

The monk takes the gospel with deepest seriousness. He is bound, by his faith in Christ, to develop a *special awareness* of the spiritual possibilities and hazards of human life. "Take heed to yourselves..." The monastic life is a life which, by means of discipline and renunciation, delivers man from the heedlessness and irresponsibility, the spiritual insensibility and the lack of freedom which comes from immersion in cares, pleasure and self-seeking.

The monk strives to learn that spirit of sacrifice by which, basing himself on trust in Christ and on faith in the nearness and power of Christ, he can let go of himself, abandon concern for his own life and his own fulfillment, in order to surrender to a deeper, invisible principle. The Holy Spirit becomes mysteriously present as a source of life and light to the man who, for love of Christ, no longer seeks to follow the guidance of his own individual caprice and his own will.

The monk strives to penetrate the deep meaning of all the words of Christ, to keep them in his heart day and night, pondering on them (Luke 2:19).

The monk seeks union with Christ by obedient and faithful love. He believes that by love he abides in Christ and Christ abides in him (John 15:1–5). This mysterious union of the Christian with Christ can and does become more than a matter of blind faith. In the monastic life, faith opens out into a spiritual light of understanding which is however proportionate to the monk's humility and purity of heart (see Matthew 5:3–12).

MONASTIC LIFE AT GETHSEMANI

A religious vocation is an inspiration of the Holy Spirit, moving a Christian to leave the world and give himself to God by a life of renunciation, according to the evangelical counsels. Vocations come from God, not from man. And this means two things: first, that merely human aspirations and drives can never constitute a religious vocation. A natural yearning for silence and seclusion will never make a Trappist. Secondly, when God calls, man has no right to place obstacles in the way of the one who is called.

An inspiration of the Holy Spirit does not mean a pious "feeling" that one is called. A person may truly be called to the monastic life and yet feel little or no sensible attraction to it. But in that case the vocation makes itself known by a peaceful, persistent conviction in the mind and a firm, steady purpose of the will. When there is a true vocation, its fulfillment always brings a deep spiritual peace to the heart of one called, even though repugnance and suffering may be present in the emotions for a while....

No one should enter a Cistercian monastery unless he is reasonably sure that he will be able, with the help of God's grace, to keep the holy vows—poverty, chastity, obedience, stability and conversion of manners. Above all, no one with nervous disorders or deep psychological conflicts should attempt to become a Trappist monk. This would prove a fatal mistake and might have very serious consequences.

The real test of a vocation to the Cistercian life is the capacity to be formed into a true monk and the aptitude to live according to the spirit of the Order. But what is the spirit of the Order?

In this expression, the word "spirit" refers to a set of attitudes and motives, a spiritual outlook, an ideal which moves and guides the monk in all that he does. The "Cistercian spirit" is simply the spiritual instinct which prompts the monk to follow Christ in the same way as St. Benedict and St. Bernard did before him. It is indeed a very special grace, the fruit of fidelity to God's call and of docility in the novitiate formation. To have a true "Cistercian spirit" is to possess a certain mode of Christ-likeness, a certain combination of virtues and spiritual gifts, which are characteristic of the monks of this Order.

To be a monk, one must first of all be an uncompromising disciple of Jesus Christ. One must practice all the virtues so dear to the Heart of Jesus, particularly the virtue of faith. One must live in an attitude of total dependence upon prayer and expect all good from the hands of a merciful God rather than from the resources of our own nature. One must have the spirit of obedience, trust, gentleness, humility, and self-denial which are required of every true religious. Above all, one must live a life of charity, without which everything else is illusion.

All this is necessary for every Christian. What is especially characteristic of the Cistercian? He loves poverty, prayer, silence, penance and he seeks solitude in community life.

The Cistercian imitates the poverty of Jesus' life at Nazareth. He withdraws from the empty noise of cities to humble his heart, his mind and his imagination before the inscrutable mystery of God.

The Cistercian spirit of prayer is the same as that which made Jesus spend whole nights on the mountainside alone with His Father. It is a spirit of adoration and contemplation which drives the monk to lose himself in the beauty and magnificence of the mystery of God.

Without penance the monk's prayer is empty. One who truly seeks God will fly from all sin, and will lament the sins of the world and his own past sins. His heart will be filled with compunction, not with morbid self-castigation, but with trusting abandonment to the mercy of God.

The Cistercian is a member of a monastic family which lives closely united in bonds of warm and whole-hearted charity. But he is also at the same time a solitary whom silence isolates in continual meditation or prayer. The true Cistercian is not divided by this paradox. He is able to be perfectly at peace in solitude and community at the same time. He feels united with his brothers, but is not preoccupied with them.

This reconciliation is not achieved by strained efforts at "recollection" but by simplicity and humble faith. The self-forgetful monk is able to see God without any need to exclude one in order to find the other. Do you seek all this? Then one thing more is necessary: *Courage.*

MONASTIC LIFE AT GETHSEMANI

*T*he whole monastic life is oriented by its intention to the love and praise of God. Everything the monk does, whether he eats or drinks or sleeps or works, reads or meditates, prays or sings, is guided by one overall intention: to praise God and to please Him, to carry out His will on earth. Hence every act of the monk becomes in some way an act of worship and an act of love. All is referred to the loving kindness of God who brought us into being out of love, in order that we may spend eternity in loving Him.

A great part of the monk's day—and night—is spent in formal worship, whether in choir and in the liturgical service of the sanctuary, or in secret and personal prayers.

Liturgy is the common worship of the monastic family, celebrating the sacred mysteries together and participating in the Lord's supper, in order to make present each day the redemptive sacrifice of Christ's death and resurrection in which the Father receives perfect praise. The daily concelebrated Mass gathers the entire community around the altar of God in a solemn and yet simple affirmation of faith and love which sums up and consecrates all the rest of the monk's activities....

In the various hours of the choral office, beginning with the Night Vigils at two thirty in the morning, the monk chants the psalms, listens to sacred readings, prays and meditates on the word of God. Thus his day is consecrated by moments set apart for singing the formal praises of God in psalms and hymns. Having adopted a rule of silence in order to speak to men only when necessary, the monk devotes his voice, tongue and heart to this one purpose above all: the praise and glory of God.

Silent and meditative prayer is also an important part of the monk's life. Here the monk prays alone and in the solitude of his heart, meditates on his reading, seeks God's will by deeply reflecting on the events and demands of his daily life, and even seeks a more ineffable personal union with God in wordless, silent prayer and in perfect self-abandonment. Here the ways of prayer become mysterious and sometimes baffling to the one who experiences them: but with faith and trust in God he pursues the way trodden before him by many of the saints, in order to be purified and illumined by grace, and united with Christ in one Spirit (1 Corinthians 6:17).

Such is the life of the monk. It is at once traditional and modern. Traditional in its essential pattern, which has been the same for centuries,

but modern in the new forms by which it seeks to
express itself in the lives of essentially modern men,
in the most technologically advanced nation on
earth.

GETHSEMANI: A LIFE OF PRAISE

The "interior" conversion that makes a monk
will usually show itself outwardly in certain ways:
obedience, humility, silence, detachment, modesty.
All of these can be summed up in one word: peace.

It is not the tranquility of a rich man's country
home. It is the peace of poor men who are
supernaturally content with their poverty, not
because it delivers them from the worries and
responsibilities of the world, nor yet because it
helps them to lead a life that is essentially healthier
and better balanced than the life of the world: but
because it inexplicably puts them in possession of
the God of all peace.

The peace of the monastic life is not to be
accounted for by a natural and human explanation.
Enter a monastery and see the life close at hand.
You will find that what looks so perfect from the
windows of the guest house is in reality full of the
seams and cracks of human imperfection. The
tempo of community life is not invariably serene.
The order of the day can sometimes become
unbalanced, surcharged, distracting as well as
exhausting. Usages and observances are sometimes

twisted into ridiculous formalities. There are moments when everything in the monastery seems to conspire to make peace and prayer impossible. These things inevitably ripple the surface of life in the best of communities. Their function is to remind us that the peace of the monks depends, ultimately, on something deep and hidden in their own souls. Monastic regularity is certainly most important in preserving peace. If regularity were to be lost forever, peace could not last long. But even where the life goes on according to rule, the rule alone is not sufficient to explain the peace of those who live by it. We must look deeper into the mystery of faith by which, in the secret recesses of their souls, the monks remain in possession of God no matter what may happen to disturb the surface of their lives.

The monastic life burns before the invisible God like a lamp before a tabernacle. The wick of the lamp is faith, the flame is charity, and the oil, by which the flame is fed, is self-sacrifice.

NO MAN IS AN ISLAND

*T*he monk is a man who has been called by the Holy Spirit to relinquish the cares, desires and ambitions of other men, and devote his entire life to seeking God. The concept is familiar. The reality which the concept signifies is a mystery. For in actual fact, no one on earth knows precisely what it means to "seek God" until he himself has set out to find Him. No man can tell another what this search means unless that other is enlightened, at the same time, by the Spirit speaking within his own heart. In the end, no one can seek God unless he has already begun to find Him. No one can find God without having first been found by Him. A monk is a man who seeks God because he has been found by God.

THE SILENT LIFE

The deepest law in man's being is his need for God, for life. God is Life. "In Him was life, and the life was the light of men, and the light shines in the darkness and the darkness comprehended it not" (John 1:5). The deepest need of our darkness is to comprehend the light which shines in the midst of it. Therefore God has given us, as His first commandment: "Thou shalt love the Lord thy God with thy whole heart, and with thy whole soul and with all thy strength." The monastic life is nothing but the life of those who have taken the first commandment in deadly earnest, and have, in the words of St. Benedict, "preferred nothing to the love of Christ."

THE SILENT LIFE

The monk is one who has heard God speak the words He spoke once through the Prophet: "I will espouse thee to me in faith, and thou shalt know that I am the Lord" (Osee [Hosea] 2:20).

God is to be "found" by the soul that is united to Him in a bond as intimate as marriage. And this bond is a union of spirits, in faith. Faith, here, means complete fidelity, the complete gift and abandonment of oneself. It means perfect trust in a hidden God. It implies submission to the gentle but inscrutable guidance of His infinitely hidden Spirit. It demands the renunciation of our own light and our own prudence and our own wisdom and of our whole "self" in order to live in and by His Spirit. "He that is joined to the Lord," says St. Paul, "is one Spirit" (1 Corinthians 6:17).

To be one with One Whom one cannot see is to be hidden, to be nowhere, to be no one: it is to be unknown as He is unknown, forgotten as He is forgotten, lost as He is lost to the world which nevertheless exists in Him. Yet to live in Him is to live by His power, to reach from end to end of the universe in the might of His wisdom, to rule and form all things in and with Him. It is to be the hidden instrument of His Divine action, the minister of His redemption, the channel of His mercy, and the messenger of His infinite Love.

THE SILENT LIFE

*H*umility detaches the monk first of all from that absorption in himself which makes him forget the reality of God. It detaches him from that fixation upon his own will which makes him ignore and disobey the eternal Will in which alone reality is to be found. [Humility] gradually pulls down the edifice of illusory projects which he has erected between himself and reality. It strips him of the garment of spurious ideals which he has woven to disguise and beautify his own imaginary self. It finds him and saves him in the midst of hopeless conflict against the rest of the universe—saves him in this conflict by a salutary "despair" in which he renounces at last his futile struggle to make himself into a "god." When he achieves this final renunciation he plunges through the center of his humility to find himself at last in the Living God.

The victory of monastic humility is the victory of the real over the unreal—a victory in which false human ideals are discarded, and the divine "ideal" is attained, is experienced, is grasped and possessed, not in a mental image but in the present, and concrete, and existential reality of our life. The victory of monastic humility is a triumph of life in which, by the integration of thought and action, idealism and reality, prayer and work, the monk finds that he now lives perfectly, and fully, and fruitfully in God. Yet God does not appear. The monk is not outwardly changed. He has no *aureola* [halo]. He is still a frail and limited human being. The externals of his life are the same as they always were. Prayer is the same, work is the same, the monastic community is the same, but everything has been changed from within and God is, to use St. Paul's expression, "all in all."

THE SILENT LIFE

*I*t must be admitted that every vocation has its professional hazards and the monk who loses sight of the meaning of his monastic calling may well waste his life in sterile preoccupation. But the meaning of the monk's flight from the world is precisely to be sought in the fact that the "world" (in the sense in which it is condemned by Christ) is the society of those who live exclusively for themselves. To leave the "world" then is to leave oneself first of all and begin to live for others. The man who lives "in the world but not of it" is one who, in the midst of life, with all its crises, forgets himself to live for those he loves. The monastery aims to create an atmosphere most favorable for selflessness. If some of the monks make a bad use of their opportunity and become selfish, it is because they have physically left "the world" while bringing its spirit with them into the monastery in their hearts. They have not come to seek God so much as their own interests, their own profit, their own peace, their own perfection.

THE SILENT LIFE

$\mathcal{M}$any details of the monk's austere life may be relaxed by his superiors. There may be modification in his daily prayer, his manual work, his fasting, his silence: but in one thing there can be no change—in the monk's fundamental obligation to be "obedient unto death." This means that he must relinquish, if not life itself, at least his stubborn will to "live" and exist as a self-assertive and self-seeking individual. To renounce the pleasure of one's deepest illusions about oneself is to die more effectively than one could ever do by allowing himself to be killed for a clearly conceived personal ideal. Indeed, we know it is quite possible for a man to lay down his life to bear witness to his own will and to his own illusions. But the true and complete renunciation of ourselves is demanded by the monastic life. Even if our superiors seek to spare our weakness, God Himself will not spare us, if we are truly seeking Him.

However, to live "under the sacrament of the Cross" is to share in the life of the Risen Christ. For when our illusions die, they give place to reality, and when our false "self" disappears, when the darkness of self-idolatry is dispelled, then the words of the Apostle are fulfilled in us: "Arise, thou that sleepest, and Christ will enlighten thee" (Ephesians 5:14).

THE SILENT LIFE

𝒜 monk is one who lives "in truth"—*dans le vrai.* His mission in life is to become so real, under the action of the Spirit of Him Who is, that his own life is a pure "amen."

Cistercian asceticism, and indeed all the asceticism of the monastic Fathers, is simply the recovery of the true self, man's true "nature," created for union with God. It is the purification and liberation of the divine image in man, hidden under the layers of "unlikeness." Our true self is the person we are meant to be—the person who is free and upright, in the image and likeness of God. The work of recovery of this lost likeness is affected by stripping away all that is alien and foreign to our true selves—shedding the "double garment" of hypocrisy and illusion by which we try to conceal the truth of our misery from ourselves, our brethren and from God.

If the monk is to build a solid and enduring temple to the glory of God—the monastic community united in perfect charity—he must first of all work at making himself real. He must discover the truth about himself. The foundation of the sacred edifice is the humility of all its living stones. Only by building on truth can we build solidly. And this means not only honesty but self-denial—the generous effort to sweep out of our lives all that is useless, all that is "alien," all that is

not willed for us by God. Only then can we be our
true selves.

THE SILENT LIFE

*T*he great ends of the monastic life can only be
seen in the light of the mystery of Christ. Christ
is the center of monastic living. He is its source
and its end. He is the way of the monk as well
as his goal. Monastic rules and observances, the
practices of monastic asceticism and prayer, must
always be integrated into this higher reality. They
must always be seen as part of a living reality,
as manifestations of a divine life rather than as
elements in a system, as manifestations of duty
alone. The monk does more than conform to edicts
and commands which he cannot understand—he
abandons his will in order to live in Christ.

THE MONASTIC JOURNEY

*T*he monk, a man of prayer, must learn that
through his prayers, through the blessing that is
spread abroad by the presence of a monastery, the
world is sanctified and brought closer to God. He
must rejoice in the fact that by his hidden union
with Christ he enables all things to come close to
their last end, and to give glory to their creator.

The monk must see the monastic community
as Christ, living, visible and present in the midst
of His creation, and blessing all the surrounding

country and all the things which the monks touch and use, leading all things to unite with us in praising God through His incarnate son. The material things which surround us are holy because of our bodies, which are sanctified by our souls, which are sanctified by the presence of the indwelling word (cf. St. Bernard [of Clairvaux's] sermons on the Dedication of a Church).

The created universe is a temple of God, in which our monastery is, as it were, the altar, the community is the tabernacle, and Jesus Himself is present in the Community, offering His homage of love and praise to the Father and sanctifying souls and all things.

Hence, in the monastic life, our senses are *educated* and elevated, rather than destroyed. But this education requires discipline. If our eyes are to be the eyes of the "new man" (Christ), they must no longer look upon things with the desires and prejudices of the "old man." They must be purified by faith, hope and love. While mortifying our senses, monastic asceticism gives them a new life in Christ, so that we learn to see, hear, feel, taste, etc., as Christ, and even our senses are then spiritualized.

THE MONASTIC JOURNEY

Christ is not just a sublime hero whom we must strive with every nerve to imitate—He is a loving savior who has come down to our level to give us His strength. He willed to identity Himself with our weakness in [the Garden of] Gethsemani and on the cross.

We seek Jesus not only as our personal, individual salvation, but as the salvation and the unity of all mankind. The original solidarity of man, on which our perfect happiness and fulfillment depend, was destroyed by sin and man cannot find peace and unity within himself, or in society, until he is reconciled to God in Christ. Christ is our peace, with one another, with ourselves, and with God. Therefore we seek Him as the savior of the world, as the Prince of Peace, who will restore the unity of mankind in his kingdom of peace.

THE MONASTIC JOURNEY

What does the Holy Spirit say to us in our reading of Scripture? He teaches us to see in Scripture the great themes which we have been treating as fundamental in the monastic life—the word made flesh, the divine redeemer uniting to Himself a "perfect people" living in Him, by His Spirit, and united through Him to the Father. More particularly, the Holy Spirit enlightens us, in our reading, to see *how our own lives* are part of these great mysteries—how we are one with Jesus in them. And then the Holy Spirit opens our eyes and attunes our hearts to the future, the consummation of all and the glory of Christ in His Church.

THE MONASTIC JOURNEY

$\mathcal{T}$he monastery is a school of charity, in which men learn love, not out of books but in the book of life itself, which is the heart of the savior, Jesus Christ. This is a living book, written not on sheets of paper but in God Himself, and reproduced in the hearts of men purified and moved by the Holy Spirit. The science of the saints, which is the main object of study in the monastery, is not learned in word but in deeds; it is not fully possessed by one who does not live it.

THE MONASTIC JOURNEY

$\mathcal{S}$t. Benedict, following the tradition of the monks of the East, proposed to his followers a life in which everything is nourished by faith and every action bears fruit in the growth of love. The first word of the Rule opens our ears to the inward promptings of the Holy Spirit: "*Ausculta!*—Listen, my son, to the precepts of the master!" Who is the master? The Gospel tells us: "one is your master, Christ" and St. Benedict himself adds," he that hath ears to hear, let him hear what the Spirit says to the Churches." The whole Benedictine life is a life of faith in the word of God, received into the faithful heart like the seed in good ground, to bring forth fruit in patience....

St. Bernard of Clairvaux expanded and implemented the thought of St. Benedict when he called the monastery a school of charity. The main object of monastic discipline, according to St. Bernard, was to restore man's nature created in the image and likeness of God, that is to say created for love and self-surrender.

Readers who have been brought up on a more recent vintage of spirituality may be surprised at St. Bernard's declaration that monastic discipline is in favor of human nature rather than against it. St. Bernard never regards human nature as evil, or as the source of evil. On the contrary, what is made by God in His own image and likeness must necessarily be a great good, and the saint declares that it is a real evil for men to ignore the good that is in themselves. Indeed, this ignorance of the good that is within us leads us into every sin, makes us resemble the beasts rather than God.

Ignorance plunges us ultimately into despair. Our first task then is to know ourselves—to know the good that is in us, to know God's love for us, so that we may reply to Him with the love of our own hearts and love Him "without measure." But at the same time we must be realistic. The divine image in us has been disfigured and mutilated by sin. What is this divine image? Our liberty, that is to say, the capacity to commit ourselves, to give ourselves, to surrender ourselves, to pay the supreme homage of our inmost being to what we have chosen as our good. One can see that in our liberty is hidden supreme power for good as well as for evil. We can dedicate our lives, in love, to truth or to falsity, to good or to evil. We can give ourselves to God or to mammon, His enemy. We can surrender to Him who is, or we can cast ourselves away with one who is not, who is only the shadow and the negation and the denial of what is.

THE MONASTIC JOURNEY

$\mathcal{I}$f we are to live as members of Christ, we are forced, by the very nature of our vocation and by the insistent demands of the Spirit of Christ, to rise above ourselves, to burst out of our own limits, and stretch out to attain something of the stature of Christ. But one who remains narrow and petty and self-centered cannot expand to embrace the whole world without feeling some strain and suffering in the process. In order to become big we must sacrifice our smallness. In order to reach out to many, we must abandon our miserable concentration upon our self, with its little needs, its demands, its whims, and its illusions.

Paradoxically, the first thing we must sacrifice, in order to become great, is our own idea of greatness. That is why St. Benedict insists that the only way to perfection is humility. Our human notions of what is "great" and "big" and "noble" are all corrupted by egoism. We find it difficult to realize that one who would be truly great must totally disappear. If our light is to shine before the world, and give glory to God, it must first of all be extinguished, then re-enkindled with the flame of the Holy Spirit.

THE MONASTIC JOURNEY

Monastic Prayer in Solitude and Silence

I am the unexpected flash
Beyond "yes," beyond "no,"
The forerunner of the Word of God.

Follow my ways and I will lead you
To golden-haired suns,
Logos and music, blameless joys,
Innocent of questions
And beyond answers:

For I, Solitude, am thine own self:
I, Nothingness, am thy All.
I, Silence, am thy Amen!

FROM "SONG: IF YOU SEEK..."
IN COLLECTED POEMS

$\mathcal{I}$ am speaking of the solitary spirit which is really essential to the monastic view of life, but which is not limited to monasteries. Nor is it limited to men and women who have consecrated their lives to God by vow. Therefore, though I am treating of the traditional concept of the *monachos* or solitary, I am deliberately discarding everything that can conjure up the artificial image of the monk in a cowl, dwelling in a medieval cloister. In this way I intend obviously, not to disparage or to reject the monastic institution, but to set aside all its accidentals and externals, so that they will not interfere with my view of what seems to me to be deepest and most essential. But by that same token,

the "solitary" of these pages is never necessarily
a "monk" (juridically) at all. He may well be a
layman, and of the sort most remote from the
cloistered life, like [Henry David] Thoreau or Emily
Dickinson.

DISPUTED QUESTIONS

*T*he early Christians who went into the desert
to see the hermits of Nitria and Scete admired in
them not so much their extreme asceticism as their
charity and discretion. The miracle of the Desert
Fathers was precisely that a man could live entirely
separate from the visible Christian community
with its normal liturgical functions, and still be
full of the charity of Christ. He was able to be so
only because he was completely empty of himself.
The vocation to solitude is therefore at the same
time a vocation to silence, poverty and emptiness.
But the emptiness is for the sake of fullness:
the purpose of the solitary life is, if you like,
contemplation. But not contemplation in the pagan
sense of an intellectual, esoteric enlightenment,
achieved by ascetic technique. The contemplation
of the Christian solitary is the awareness of the
divine mercy transforming and elevating his own
emptiness and turning it into the presence of
perfect love, perfect fullness.

DISPUTED QUESTIONS

A Catholic contemplative instinctively seeks something more than the testimony of individual mystics and saints about their experience of God. Catholic contemplation is essentially founded on dogmatic truth. It is more than a quest for the Absolute which can be satisfied by appropriate techniques of recollection. The Catholic mystic seeks, above all, the mind and truth of God. And he seeks it in the word of God. If he withdraws from the world and stands at the frontiers of eternity, it is because he somehow hopes to see God, or at least to hear His voice. If he calls out to God in prayer, it is because he desires an answer. And the answer he desires is not merely the voice of his own fancy, or the echo of another human experience like his own. It must be God's answer.

BREAD IN THE WILDERNESS

*O*ne of the first essentials of the interior solitude of which I speak is that it is the actualization of a faith in which a man takes responsibility for his own inner life. He faces its full mystery, in the presence of the invisible God. And he takes upon himself the lonely, barely comprehensible, incommunicable task of working his way through the darkness of his own mystery until he discovers that his mystery and the mystery of God merge into one reality, which is the only reality. That God lives in him and he in God—not precisely in the way that words seems to suggest (for words have no power to comprehend that reality) but in a way that makes words, and even attempts to communicate, seem utterly illusory.

The words of God, the words which unite in "One Body" the society of those who truly believe, have the power to signify the mystery of our loneliness and oneness in Christ, to point the way into its darkness. They have the power, also, to illuminate the darkness. But they do so by losing the shape of words and becoming—not thoughts, not things, but the unspeakable beating of a Heart within the heart of one's own life.

DISPUTED QUESTIONS

*T*he lone man remains in the world as a prophet to whom no one listens, as a voice crying in the desert, as a sign of contradiction. The world necessarily rejects him and in that act, rejects the dreaded solitude of God Himself. For that is what the world resents about God: His utter otherness, His absolute incapacity to be absorbed into the context of worldly and practical slogans, His mysterious transcendence which places Him infinitely beyond the reach of catchwords, advertisements and politics. It is easier for the world to recreate a god in its own image, a god who justifies its own slogans, when there are no solitaries about to remind men of the solitude of God: the God Who cannot become a member of any purely human fellowship. And yet this Solitary God has called men to another fellowship, with Himself, through the Passion and Resurrection of Christ—through the solitude of Gethsemani and of Calvary, and the mystery of Easter, and the solitude of the Ascension: all of which precede the great communion of Pentecost.

The lonely man's function is to remain in existence as solitary, as poor and as unacceptable as God Himself in the souls of so many men. The solitary is there to tell them, in a way they can barely understand, that if they were able to discover and appreciate their own inner solitude they would immediately discover God and find out, from His word to them, that they are really persons.

DISPUTED QUESTIONS

Without solitude of some sort there is and can be no maturity. Unless one becomes empty and alone, he cannot give himself in love because he does not possess the deep self which is the only gift worthy of love. And this deep self, we immediately add, cannot be *possessed*. My deep self is not "something" which I acquire, or to which I "attain" after a long struggle. It is not mine, and cannot become mine. It is no "thing"—no object. It is "I."

The shallow "I" of individualism can be possessed, developed, cultivated, pandered to, satisfied: it is the center of all our strivings for gain and for satisfaction, whether material or spiritual. But the deep "I" of the spirit, of solitude and of love, cannot be "had," possessed, developed, perfected. It can only *be*, and *act* according to deep inner laws which are not of man's contriving, but which come from God. They are the Laws of the Spirit, who, like the wind, blows where He wills. This inner "I," who is always alone, is always universal: for in this inmost "I" my own solitude meets the solitude of every other man and the solitude of God. Hence it is beyond division, beyond limitation, beyond selfish affirmation. It is only this inmost and solitary "I" that truly loves with the love and the spirit of Christ. This "I" is Christ Himself, living in us: and we, in Him, living in the Father.

DISPUTED QUESTIONS

Contemplation is a gift of God in which the soul, purified by His infused love, suddenly and inexplicably experiences the presence of God within itself. This experiential recognition of God springs from the fact that pure charity has reformed the likeness to God which makes our soul like a mirror created only to reflect Him. Because contemplation is produced through the grace of an intimate union with Christ, Who is the Son of God by nature, it is essentially a full and mature participation of His divine Sonship.

In contemplation, we know God formally as our "Father," that is to say not only as our Creator in the natural order, but as the living and intimately active source of our supernatural life as well. Contemplation is our personal response to His mystical presence and activity within us. We suddenly realize that we are confronted with the infinitely rich source of all Being and all Love, and although we do not literally "see" Him, for our meeting takes place in the dark night of faith, yet there is something in the deepest center of our being, something at the very spiritual apex of our life, that leaps with elation at this contact with the Being of Him who is almighty. The spark that is struck within us by this touch of the finger of God kindles a sheet of flame that goes forth to proclaim His presence in every fiber of our being and to praise Him from the marrow of our bones.

BREAD IN THE WILDERNESS

The truly solitary life has a completely different character from the partial solitude which can be enjoyed from time to time in the intervals allowed by social living. When we receive our solitude by intervals, we taste its value by contrast with another value. When we really live alone, there is no contrast.

I must not go into solitude to immobilize my life, to reduce all things to a frozen concentration upon some inner experience. When solitude alternates with common living, it can take on this character of a halt, of a moment of stillness, an interval of concentration. Where solitude is not an interval but a continuous whole, we may well renounce altogether the sense of concentration and feeling of spiritual stillness. Our whole life may flow out to meet the Being and the Silence of the days in which we are immersed, and we can work out our salvation by quiet, continued action.

It is even possible that in solitude I shall return to my beginning and rediscover the value and perfection of simple vocal prayer—and take greater joy in this than in contemplation.

THOUGHTS IN SOLITUDE

The monk who is truly a man of prayer and who seriously faces the challenge of his vocation in all its depth is by that very fact exposed to existential dread. He experiences in himself the emptiness, the lack of authenticity, the quest for fidelity, the "lostness" of modern man, but he experiences all this in an altogether different and deeper way than does man in the modern world, to whom this disconcerting awareness of himself and of his world comes rather as an experience of boredom and spiritual disorientation. The monk confronts his own humanity and that of his world at the deepest and most central point where the void seems to open out into black despair. The monk confronts this serious possibility, and rejects it, as Camusian man confronts "the absurd" and transcends it by his freedom. The option of absolute despair is turned into perfect hope by the pure and humble supplication of monastic prayer. The monk faces the worst, and discovers in it the hope of the best. From the darkness comes light. From death, life. From the abyss there comes, unaccountably, the mysterious gift of the Spirit sent by God to make all things new, to transform the created and redeemed world, and to re-establish all things in Christ.

This is the creative and healing work of the monk, accomplished in silence, in nakedness of spirit, in emptiness, in humility. It is a participation in the saving death and resurrection of Christ. Therefore every Christian may, if he so desires, enter into communion with this silence of the praying and meditating Church, which is the Church of the Desert.

CONTEMPLATIVE PRAYER

What is it that makes every man struggle with himself? It is the deep, persistent voice of his own discontent with himself. Fallen man cannot abide to live with himself. Now the apparent peace which the world gives is bought with the price of continual distraction. Distraction merely drowns out the inner voice, it does not answer any questions, or solve any problems, it merely postpones their solution. And behind the smokescreen of amusements and projects, the inner dissatisfaction marshals all its forces for a more terrible assault when the distraction shall have been taken away. At last, the spirit that has fled from itself all its life is stripped of its distractions at death and finds itself face to face with what can no longer be avoided: there is nothing now to prevent if from hating itself utterly, and totally, and forever.

The peace which Christ brings is the outcome of this war faced and fought on earth: man's war with himself, in which (by God's grace) he overcomes himself, conquers himself, pacifies himself, and can at last live with himself because he no longer hates himself. But this conquest of himself can never be definitive unless it is a surrender to another: to Christ, and to our brother in Christ. For our destiny is to be one in Christ, and in order to love others as ourselves, we must first love ourselves. But in order to love ourselves we must find something in ourselves to love. This is impossible unless we find, both in ourselves and in others, the likeness of Christ.

In order to find Christ we must give up our own limited idea of Christ. He is not what we think He is. His is not, and cannot be, merely our own idealized image of ourselves....

We must learn to listen to what goes on in our

heart and interpret it correctly. We will never find peace if we listen to the voice of our own fatuous self-deception that tells us the conflict has ceased to exist. We will find peace when we can listen to the "death dance in our blood" not only with equanimity but with exultation because we hear within it the echoes of the victory of the Risen Savior.

Only in this proper understanding of ourselves can we come to that true compunction which is the very heart of monastic prayer. How shall we sing *Lord have Mercy* if our eyes have never been opened to our need for mercy? But what will be the rending of our heart when we recognize that it is Christ Himself, in us, who cries out for mercy—and that He cries not only to the Father, but to us. Yes, it is Christ Himself who has identified Himself with us and begs us to begin by having mercy on ourselves, not now for our own sake but for His! Such is the love of God for us, so great is its mystery, and so far beyond the capacity of our hearts to comprehend! He who could have punished us, instead forgives us. But His is a strange way of forgiveness: He identifies Himself with us and asks us, as it were, to begin by forgiving ourselves. In doing this for Him, we are, as it were, forgiving Him. If we forgive Him, He forgives us. Then He gives us peace with ourselves—because we are at peace with Him....

The secret of monastic peace is therefore not

to be sought on the shallow level of psychological tranquility, but in the infinitely deep abyss which men call the divine mercy.

THE MONASTIC JOURNEY

*O*ur growth in Christ is measured not only by intensity of love but also by the deepening of our vision, for we begin to see Christ now not only in our own deep souls, not only in the Psalms, not only in the Mass, but everywhere, shining to the Father in the features of men's faces. The more we are united to Him in love, the more we are united in love to one another, because there is only one charity embracing both God and our [neighbor].

In this union we discover, and the conviction gains more and more power as we are emptied of selfishness by suffering, that there is so to speak "One mystical Person," after all, chanting the Psalms. It is no longer we alone who pronounce the words of David or of some long-dead Jew. It is the eternal Christ. He is "chanting the Psalms in heaven," because His glorified Humanity is the center of their Mysteries and the life of all who enter into these mysteries. All we who are members of His Body are one in Him and one with Him.

BREAD IN THE WILDERNESS

The monastic life cannot be defined by any one of its parts. It cannot be reduced to one of its aspects, any more than the life of any living organism can be fully explained by one of the vital functions which that organism performs. Man is a rational animal, they say. But he does not exist merely in order to grow, or eat, or work, or think, or even to love. On the contrary, growth, nutrition, work, thought and love all unite in promoting and increasing the existential depth of the mysterious reality which is the individual person, a concrete, free, inexplicable being endowed with powers whose depth no mind but God's can ever fathom. The human person, then, is a free being created with capacities that can only be fulfilled by the vision of an unknown God. And the monk is a person who has been unable to resist the need to seek this unknown God in the hiddenness and silence of His own inscrutable wisdom.

All the substance of the monastic vocation, therefore, is buried in the silence where God and the soul meet, not as object and subject, but as "one Spirit." The very essence of monasticism is hidden in the existential darkness of life itself. And life is inexplicable, irreducible to systematic terms. It is only understood by being lived. The best we can say is that the monk is one who goes out to the frontiers of liberty and of existence, seeking the impossible, seeking the vision which no man can see without dying. And yet this idea must immediately be corrected, for it is at once exaggerated and misleading. For when the monk is able to reach a certain degree of wisdom, he realizes that he had already found God by becoming mysteriously unwise. And then the circle is closed, and the monastic life begins.

SILENCE IN HEAVEN

*W*hether in the cloister or in the hermitage, the monk's vocation is always a call to sink deep roots in the silence of God. The spirit that lives in that immense silence, although it may be content with the fact that the silence cannot be explained, is nevertheless free to meditate on its tremendous reality. If we cannot grasp the whole substance of the mystery, we can still catch glimpses of its hidden depths. These glances into the abyss fill the heart of the monk with joy. They deliver him still further from preoccupation with himself and other men. They turn his eyes to the manifestations of the mystery of God, the "great works" by which God has secretly entered into the stream of time in order to signify His mysterious purposes for mankind. Like all other Christians, the monk is "in God" only by being "in Christ." The silence by which he lives is the silence in which the Word comes down from His heavenly throne to accomplish the work of His Mystery. The song which he hears in silence is the voice of the Spirit of Christ, crying out in the depths of his heart "Abba, Father" (Romans 8:15).

Since he is always reciting the Psalms and reading the Scriptures the monk cannot help being penetrated with the reality of this Mystery in whose heart he is living. It is the Mystery of Christ, Who has united mankind to Himself, and purified it of sin, and raised it up to the Father. It is the Mystery of the Son of God living in the soul that knows itself to have been, and still to be in some measure a sinner. The voice of silence always speaks to the monk reminding him that he is a lost thing that is sought and found, a perishing thing that is rescued and brought home to safety, and that there exists a world to be saved together with him.

SILENCE IN HEAVEN

THE MONK IN THE
MODERN WORLD

Teach me to take all grace
And spring it into blades of act,
Grow spears and sheaves of charity,
While each new instant, (new eternity)
Flowering with clean and individual circumstance,
Speaks me the whisper of His consecrating Spirit.
Then will obedience bring forth new Incarnations
Shining to God with the features of His Christ.

"CANTICLE FOR THE BLESSED VIRGIN,"
IN COLLECTED POEMS

The monastic life today stands over against the world with a mission to affirm not only the message of salvation but also those most basic human values which the world most desperately needs to regain: personal integrity, inner peace, authenticity, identity, inner depth, spiritual joy, the capacity to love, the capacity to enjoy God's creation and give thanks....

Our first task is to be fully human....There is no need for a community of religious robots without minds, without hearts, without ideas and without faces. It is this mindless alienation that characterizes "the world" and life in the world. Monastic spirituality today must be a personalistic and Christian humanism that seeks and saves man's intimate truth, his personal identity, in order to consecrate it entirely to God.

CONTEMPLATION IN A WORLD OF ACTION

The charism of the monastic vocation is one of simplicity and truth. The monk, whether as hermit or as cenobite, is one who abandons the routines, the clichés, the disguised idolatries and empty formalities of "the world" in order to seek the most authentic and essential meaning of the dedicated life on earth. Ideally speaking, then, the monastery should be a place of utter sincerity, without empty and deceptive formalities, without evasions, without pretenses.

CONTEMPLATION IN A WORLD OF ACTION

A monk must understand the motives which have brought him to the monastery, and he must re-examine them from time to time as he grows in his vocation. But a defensive, apologetic attitude is not in accordance with the monastic life. A monk would be out of character if he tried to argue everybody into admitting that his life is justified. He expects to be taken as he is, judged for what he is, because he does not waste time trying to convince others or even himself that he amounts to anything very special.

The monk is not concerned with himself so much as with God, and with all who are loved by God. He does not seek to justify himself by comparing himself favorably with other people: rather, he sees himself and all men together in the light of great and solemn facts which no one can evade. The fact of inevitable death which puts an end to the struggles and joys of life. The fact that the meaning of life is usually obscure and sometimes seemingly impenetrable. The fact that happiness seems to elude more and more people as the world itself becomes more prosperous, more comfortable, more confident of its own powers. The fact of sin, that cancer of the spirit, which destroys not only the individual and his chances for happiness, but whole communities and even nations. The fact of human conflict, fate, aggression, destruction, subversion, deceit, the unscrupulous use of power. The fact that men who refuse to believe in God, because they think that belief is "unreasonable," do in fact surrender without reason to baser forms of faith: they believe blindly in every secular myth, whether it be racism, communism, nationalism, or one of a thousand others which men accept today without question.

The monk confronts these perplexing facts. And he confronts the religious void in the modern world. He is well aware that for many men, as for a certain philosopher (Nietzsche), "God is dead." He knows that this apparent "death" of God is in fact an expression of a disturbing modern phenomenon, the apparent inability of man to believe, the death of supernatural faith. He knows that the seeds of this death are in himself, for though he is a believer, he too sometimes must confront, in himself, the possibility of infidelity and failure. More than anyone else he realizes that faith is a pure gift of God, and that no virtue can give man room for boasting in the sight of God.

What is this so-called "death of God"? It is in fact the death of certain vital possibilities in man himself. It is the death of spiritual courage which in spite of all the denials and protestations of commonplace thinking, dares to commit itself irrevocably to belief in a divine principle of life. It is the seeming death of all capacity to conceive this as a valid possibility, to reach out to it, grasp it, to obey the promptings of the Spirit of divine life, and surrender our heart and mind to the Gospel of Jesus Christ.

THE MONASTIC JOURNEY

*R*eal sincerity with ourselves is sometimes brutally discouraging. Even though we may really want to be sincere, we have an almost infinite resourcefulness in lying to ourselves.

The effort to be sincere keeps us face to face with our own inner contradictions. It makes it impossible for us to escape the conflict, the division within us. And this division keeps us in a state of constant anguish. The paradox that one must face, if he really takes the truth seriously, is the pragmatic fact that sincerity means insecurity. If we recognize how basic is the conflict within our hearts, we cannot settle down and take roots and become "installed" on this earth. We will know the meaning of deep, bitter and even anguished insecurity. But we will also come to know the value of this insecurity: it is, in fact, the guarantee of our sincerity. It is, paradoxically, the sign that we are on the right road. It tells us that we are moving forward in the only direction possible for a Christian, and that we are in contact with reality.

Only when we become able to accept the basic contradictions in our own self, can we have the humility to understand the contradictions in others and in society. For even in the Church herself, the perfect society, there are contradictions—the everlasting distinction between wheat and cockle, with its attendant insecurity for all. No man among us can declare with assurance that he is wheat rather than cockle, and not one of us can assert that he, as opposed to "those others," represents the Church in all her purity.

In the monastic school of charity, we learn to bear one another's burdens, and precisely the greatest burden of all is this burden of insecurity and interior conflict. The first thing of all that we must face is the obligation to bear this burden and to bear it in common, but in such a way that no one is able to abdicate his own liberty and responsibility.

A school of charity, if it is a school of true charity, is also a school of freedom. It is for mature and responsible men, and not for children who have decided to leave their burden of responsibilities on the shoulders of another. A monastery is then (or at least should be) a place where man learns to bear the weight of his own freedom, and to enable others to stand up under the burden of their freedom also. Freedom is, after all, heavy to us until we become strong enough to bear it....

The "renunciation" of freedom made by the monk is a sacrifice of a lower and more material kind of autonomy in order to attain to a higher and more spiritual autonomy—the autonomy of one who is so closely united to the Holy Spirit that the Spirit of God moves him as his own spirit. "For he that is joined to the Lord in one Spirit...I live, now not I, but Christ liveth in me" [1 Corinthians 6:17; Galatians 2:20].

Such a one must dare to understand the frightening dictum of St. Augustine: "Love, and do what you will." Great is the risk involved, but it is the risk involved in true perfection—the risk that has to be faced by one who is determined in all things to be moved by nothing but the love of God.

THE MONASTIC JOURNEY

Only where the infinite truth, pity and freedom of God live in the heart of man can there be any effective social cooperation in striving for justice and truth on earth. The monk, who abandons himself to the love of God, who takes upon himself responsibility for the sins of all and holds himself responsible to all, by that very fact places himself below all, recognizes himself as worse than all, and spiritually "washes the feet" of everyone in the world—principally of those with whom he lives. In the soul of such a one there is such great meekness, such humility, such mercy, such self-effacement, such power of love, such freedom and such joy in God that his very presence brings the Holy Spirit to the hearts of men, and delivers them from sin, and shows them the way to repentance and joy in a change of heart.

Christ alone is able to bring true peace to the hearts of men, and it is through the hearts of other men that he brings it. We are all mediators for one another with Christ by our charity, by our sharing in His cross, by our love and humility in taking upon ourselves the sins of the world without condemning sinners, placing ourselves below others and forgiving all. By our humility and charity Christ lives in the world, and prepares the consummation of His kingdom, inviting men to be merciful to one another, to be just, to give every man the good that is owing to him and more besides—to repay evil with good. If all men will not hear His invitation, there must still be some in the world who will bear the sins and injustices of all, and repair them by their love. If God's justice is not visible in civil society, at least it must appear in His Church, and in His monasteries, and woe to the monastery whose monks are not felt, by the disinherited, to be their brothers.

THE MONASTIC JOURNEY

The monk is not defined by his task, his usefulness. In a certain sense he is supposed to be "useless" because his mission is not to *do* this or that job but to *be* a man of God. He does not live in order to exercise a special function: his business is life itself. This means that monasticism aims at the cultivation of a certain *quality* of life, a level of awareness, a depth of consciousness, an area of transcendence and of adoration which are not usually possible in an active secular existence....

What the monastic life should provide, then, is a special awareness and perspective, an authentic understanding of God's presence in the world and His intentions for man.

CONTEMPLATION IN A WORLD OF ACTION

The monastic life itself has retained its primitive validity, or can easily recover it, where the basic principles of the life are respected. Where there is a genuine life of solitude, poverty, prayer, silence, penance, work, charity, obedience: where the Law of the Gospel, which is a law of love and grace, is fully and fervently kept and not obscured by legalism and sermonizing, it will be easy to see that here is a way of authenticity and truth in which man does not merely discover and assert a private identity, a "personality" in the sense of a successful role, but learns that the truest way to find himself is to lose the self he has found in Christ.

CONTEMPLATION IN A WORLD OF ACTION

St. Paul long ago remarked on the obvious analogy between the training of athletes and the discipline of Christian self-denial. Over the course of long ages of routine understanding, Paul's analogy was somewhat materialized and his self-denial came to be regarded, by those who thought only superficially, as a matter of "payment" for an ultimate commodity: beatitude. This materialistic view of sacrifices as *quid pro quo*, for which one would "collect" in the afterlife, influenced the nineteenth-century view of Christian asceticism in monasteries. But really, there is more to it than that. If one "trains" and disciplines his faculties and his whole being, it is in order to deepen and expand their capacity for experience, for awareness, for understanding, for a higher kind of life, a deeper and more authentic life "in Christ" and "in the Spirit." The purpose of discipline is not only moral perfection (development of virtue for its own sake) but self-transcendence, transformation in Christ "from glory to glory as by the Spirit of the Lord." The death and crucifixion of the old self, the routine man of self-seeking and conventionally social life, leads to the resurrection in Christ of a totally "new man" who is "one Spirit" with Christ. This new man is not just the old man in possession of a legal certificate entitling him to a reward. He is no longer the same, and his reward is precisely this transformation that makes him no longer the isolated subject of a limited reward but "one with Christ" and, in Christ, with all men. The purpose of discipline is then not only to help us "turn on" and understand the inner dimensions of existence, but to transform us in Christ in such a way that we completely transcend our routine existence. (Yet in transcending it we rediscover its existential value and solidity. Transformation is not a repudiation of ordinary life but its definitive recovery in Christ.)

Monastic discipline and freedom are correlatives. In traditional ascetic terms our passions, appetites, needs, emotions, create certain limitations which hamper and frustrate a certain kind of development if we allow ourselves to remain too dependent on them. They blind us, weaken us, unnerve us, make us cowards, conformists, hypocrites. They are roots of bad faith. The craving for a certain kind of comfort, reassurance and diversion can be satisfied only if one is willing to accept certain social conditions, to fulfill a prescribed role, to occupy a definite place in society, to live according to acceptable norms. If we fulfill the role imposed on us by others, we will be rewarded by approval. These roles impose definite limitations, but in return for accepting the limitations, we enjoy the consolation of companionship, of understanding, support and so on. We are made to feel that we "belong" and are therefore "all right." The monastic idea originally was to explore the possibilities that were opened up once these limitations were removed, that is to say, once we "left the world." The comforts and joys of ordinary social life, married love, friendly converse and recreation among other people, business, a place in the city and the nation, were to some extent renounced. Sometimes the renunciation was made in crude terms, as if ordinary social life were "evil." This must not mislead us. It was simply a question of obscurely realizing that, in some way, the limitations imposed by social life stood in the way of something else, and the monk was one who wanted to look into this "something else."

The monastic life has always had something of

this element of "exploration" about it (at least in periods when it was *alive*). The monk is a man who, in one way or other, pushes to the very frontiers of human experience and strives to go beyond, to find out what transcends the ordinary level of existence. Aware that man is somehow sustained by a deep mystery of silence, of incomprehensibility—of God's will and God's love—the monk feels that he is personally called to live in more intimate communication with that mystery. And he also feels that if does not respond to this summons, he cannot be happy because he cannot be fully honest with himself. To evade this would be to reject a certain kind of truth, a certain inner reality, and ultimately to forfeit his self-respect as a human being.

I am simply trying to translate into more modern terms the familiar idea that has hitherto been expressed in the words "a monastic vocation" or "a contemplative vocation." The idea of this vocation is not necessarily confined to one special kind of discipline. There may be various different ways. Different aspects of training may be emphasized: now community life, now solitude; now ascesis, now work; now *lectio*, now silent prayer; now liturgy, now meditation; now a thoroughly sacramental piety, and now a life of spiritual risk outside the cadres of ritual and institution. But all these, some more and some less, are oriented to a kind of exploration "beyond frontiers." The claim of a cenobitic and liturgical monasticism is that it is safer and more universal because it does not push the frontiers too far and maintains a more normal human (social) measure. Yet the cenobium itself is a little Church, a sacred community, in which the Lord is present to His own in the breaking of the bread. The frontiers are dissolved, not from our side but from His. And of course this is a universal truth underlying all the paradoxes about "monastic exploration." In the end, there really are no frontiers. We could not seek God unless He were not already "in us," and to go "beyond ourselves" is just to find the inner ground of our being where He is present to us as our creative source, as the fount of redemptive light and grace. Whether as hermit or as cenobite, as pilgrim or as laborer, as hesychast or liturgist, the monk seeks in some way to respond to the summons: "Behold the Bridegroom comes: go out to meet Him!" [Matthew 25:6]. The need for discipline is the same need for watchfulness, for readiness, as in the parable. The ones who wait for the Lord must have oil in their lamps and the lamps must be trimmed. That is what monastic discipline is all about. It implies the cultivation of certain inner conditions of awareness, of openness, of readiness for the new and the unexpected. Specifically, it implies an openness to and a readiness for what is

not normally to be found in an existence where
our attention is dissipated and exhausted in other
things.

𝒯oday a new and more biblical understanding of
the contemplative life is called for: we must see it as
a response to the dynamic Word of God in history,
we must see it in the light of biblical eschatology.
The contemplative finds God not in the embrace
of "pure love" alone but in the prophetic ardor of
response to the "Word of the Lord": not in love
considered as essential good but in love that breaks
through in the world of sinful men in the fire of
judgment and mercy. The contemplative must see
love not only as the highest and purest experience
of the human heart transformed by grace, but as
God's unfailing fidelity to unfaithful man. The
contemplative life is not only Eros (the yearning of
the human heart for the vision of beauty), but also
Agape (surrender to the inexplicable mercy which
comes to us from God entirely on his own terms,
in the context of our personal and social history).
Once this has been said, Eros cannot be excluded.
However, it remains always secondary.

God speaks to us not only in the Bible, not
only in the secret inspirations of our hearts, but
also through the public and manifest events of our
own time, and above all through the Church. The

radical change in the Church's attitude toward the modern world was one of the significant events that marked Vatican II. In the light of the Council it is no longer possible to take a completely negative view of the modern world. It is no longer possible, even for contemplatives, to simply shut out the world, to ignore it, to forget it, in order to relish the private joys of contemplative Eros. To insist on the cultivation of total recollection for the sake of this Eros and its consolations would be pure and simple selfishness. It would also mean a failure to really deepen the true Christian dimensions of Agape which are the real dimension of the contemplative life.

CONTEMPLATION IN A WORLD OF ACTION

The life of solitude and contemplation, a life in which men listen more intently to the Word of God, immerse themselves in meditation of the Bible, sing the praise of God in liturgy, and devote themselves to work, study and silent prayer, is not a life remote from contemporary reality. Nor is the contemplative exempt from the problems and difficulties of contemporary man. The life of Christian contemplation is not a life of willful concentration upon a few clear and comforting ideas, but a life of inner struggle in which the monk, like Christ himself in the desert, is tested. In a certain sense the monk, alone with God, fully aware of his own poverty, fallibility and blindness, suffers the same trial of faith as other Christians, and suffers it in a more acute and penetrating way. It can be said that the contemplative is often less a "professional of vision" than a professional of crisis and intellectual suffering. What he learns is not a clearer idea of God but a deeper trust, a purer love and a more complete abandonment to One he knows to be beyond all understanding. Yet in his silence, his simple life, his cloistered peace, the contemplative certainly has access to values which modern life tends more and more to forget, to underestimate or to ignore. He wishes to share his experience of these values with other men who are weary of the pressure, the confusion, the agitation of modern life. He recognizes his duty to his fellow man: a duty to preserve for him an area which is most threatened in the stormy existence of a world in a crisis of growth and transformation.

CONTEMPLATION IN A WORLD OF ACTION

The monastic life is not only contemplative but prophetic. That is to say, it bears witness not only to a contemplative mystique of silence, enclosure and the renunciation of active works, but it is alive with the eschatological mystery of the kingdom already shared and realized in the lives of those who have heard the Word of God and have surrendered unconditionally to its demands in a vocation that (even when communal) has a distinctly "desert" quality. This suggests that there is something of a charism in every monastic vocation and in the monastic witness itself. But this does not preclude study and theological understanding. On the contrary, it presupposes a thirst for the Word of God, a willingness to immerse oneself in meditation of the Bible, in a fruitful life of prayer and celebration which is not mechanical and punctilious, but full of spontaneity and intuitive understanding. Christian wisdom and understanding must grow and deepen from day to day in the life of the monk. The whole life of the monk is a pilgrimage to the sources of Christian truth.

CONTEMPLATION IN A WORLD OF ACTION

We come to the cloister to surrender ourselves to Christ and to his Spirit in a kind of death, in order to live again in a life which he gives us. The freedom that we seek in the cloister is the freedom to be open to the new life which comes from Christ, the freedom to follow his Spirit. We seek a virginal freedom to follow the bridegroom wherever he goes, to be attentive to his every inspiration and to listen to the personal message that he has for us. This can come to us from no other source except from him speaking in our hearts. The institution of a certain kind of strict cloistered and solitary life is aimed precisely to protect this inner atmosphere of silence, listening and freedom in which Christ can do in us the work he wishes to do.

The root of our penance is faith. The root of our life of *metanoia* is a real faith in Christ, a real faith in our vocation, a real faith in the transforming power of the cross, a faith in God's promises, a faith that if we give up ourselves and our ambitions, even our spiritual ambitions, if we deliver ourselves utterly and totally into the hand of Christ and to his love, we will indeed be transformed in his time, in his way, by his Spirit. Not in our time, not in our way, and not by our own spirit.

We do not come here to be transformed by our own will and our own spirit. We come here to make this complete surrender in faith. Whether we go by the old way or by the new way, this faith is radically and urgently and critically the most important thing. This is what we have to cultivate and this is what we have, above all, to pray for.

CONTEMPLATION IN A WORLD OF ACTION

THE MONK'S
TRANSPARENCY TO
FRIENDS AND READERS

Under the blunt pine
I who am not sent
Remain. The pathway dies,
The journey has begun.
Here the bird abides
And sings on top of the forgotten
Storm. The ground is warm.
He sings no particular message.
His hymn has one pattern, no more planned,
No less perfectly planned
And no more arbitrary
Than the pattern in the seed, the salt,
The snow, the cell, the drop of rain.

"ELIAS—VARIATIONS ON A THEME,"
IN COLLECTED POEMS

*O*ne thing I know—that it is my destiny to be a contemplative, a Christian and an American. I can satisfy my vocation with nothing that is partial or provincial. I cannot be a "North American" who knows only the rivers, the plains, the mountains and the cities of the north, the north where there are few Indians, where the land was colonized and cultivated by the Puritan, where, under the audacious and sarcastic splendor of the skyscrapers, one rarely sees the Cross and where the Holy Virgin, when she is represented at all, is pale and melancholy and carries no child in her arms. This north is grand, powerful, rich, intelligent; it has a warmth of its own, a surprising humility, a charity, an inner purity which the stranger does not know. But it is incomplete. It is neither the better nor the richer part of the hemisphere. It is perhaps, at this point in time, the most important region of the world, but it is, nonetheless, not sufficient in itself and lacks the fundamental roots. It lacks the roots of the old America, the America of Mexico and the Andes, where silent and contemplative Asians came, millenniums ago, to construct their hieratic cities. It lacks the intense fervor and fecundity of Brazil, which is also African, which smiles with the grin of the Congo and laughs with the childlike innocence of Portugal. The northern half of this New World lacks the force, the refinement, the prodigality of Argentina with all the lyricism of its tormented and generous heart.

I cannot be a partial American and I cannot be, which is even sadder, a partial Catholic. For me Catholicism is not confined to one culture, one nation, one age, one race. My faith is not a mixture of the Irish Catholicism of the United States and the splendid and vital Catholicism, reborn during the last war, of my native France. Though I admire the cathedrals and the past of Catholicism in Latin America, my Catholicism goes beyond the Spanish tradition. I cannot believe that Catholicism is tied to the destinies of any group which confusedly expresses the economic illusions of a social class. My Catholicism is not the religion of the bourgeoisie nor will ever be. My Catholicism is all the world and all ages. It dates from the beginning of the world. The first man was the image of Christ and contained Christ, even as he was created, as savior in his heart. The first man was destined to be the ancestor of the Redeemer and the first woman was the mother of all life, in the image of the Immaculate Daughter who was full of grace, Mother of mercy, Mother of the saved.

Honorable Reader

*M*any rumors have been disseminated about me since I came to the monastery. Most of them have assured people that I had left the monastery, that I had returned to New York, that I was in Europe, that I was in South America or Asia, that I had become a hermit, that I was married, that I was drunk, that I was dead.

I am still in the monastery, and intend to stay there. I have never had any doubt whatever of my monastic vocation. If I have ever had any desire to change, it has been for a more solitary, more "monastic" way. But precisely because of this it can be said that I am in some sense everywhere. My monastery is not a home. It is not a place where I am rooted and established in the earth. It is not an environment in which I become aware of myself as an individual, but rather a place in which I disappear from the world as an object of interest in order to be everywhere in it by hiddenness and compassion. To exist everywhere I have to be No-one.

But the monastery is not an "escape" from the world. On the contrary, by being in the monastery I take my true part in all the struggles and sufferings of the world. To adopt a life that is essentially nonassertive, nonviolent, a life of humility and peace is in itself a statement of one's position. But each one in such a life can, by the personal modality of his decision, give his whole life a special orientation. It is my intention to make my entire life a rejection of, a protest against the crimes and injustices of war and political tyranny which threaten to destroy the whole race of man and the world with him. By my monastic life and vows I am saying "NO" to all the concentration camps, the aerial bombardments, the staged political trials, the judicial murders, the racial injustices, the economic tyrannies, and the whole socioeconomic apparatus which seems geared for nothing but global destruction in spite of all its fair words in favor of peace. I make monastic silence a protest against the lies of politicians, propagandists and agitators, and when I speak it is to deny that my faith and my Church can ever seriously be aligned with these forces of injustice and destruction. But it is true, nevertheless, that the faith in which I believe is also invoked by many who believe in war, believe in racial injustices, believe in self-righteousness and lying forms of tyranny. My life must, then, be a protest against these also, and perhaps against these most of all.

$\mathcal{I}$ will be very glad to say Masses for all the intentions sent in to me as soon as possible. Be sure that I keep all these needs you have mentioned in my prayers and think often of all these problems: God knows, you are by no means alone. Most of you, even with all that you have to suffer, are much better off than you realize. Yet the heart of man can be full of so much pain, even when things are exteriorly "all right." It becomes all the more difficult because today we are used to thinking that there are explanations for everything. But there is no explanation for most of what goes on in our own hearts, and we cannot account for it all. No use resorting to the kind of mental tranquillizers that even religious explanations sometimes offer. Faith must be deeper than that, rooted in the unknown and in the abyss of darkness that is the ground of our being. No use teasing the darkness to try to make answers grow out of it. But if we learn how to have a deep inner patience, things solve themselves, or God solves them if you prefer; but do not expect to see how. Just learn to wait, and do what you can and help other people. Often in helping someone else we find the best way to bear our own trouble.

My prayers are with you in the New Year. Pray for me. Pray for peace, because people need it and because violence will lead inevitably to the establishment of tyranny in one form or another. Pray for freedom both for those who know they are not free and especially for those who think they are free and do not realize they are prisoners of dead ideas and prejudices.

CIRCULAR LETTER TO FRIENDS:
"CHRISTMAS MORNING—1966," IN *THE ROAD TO JOY*

*M*ore and more since living alone I have wanted to stop fighting and arguing, and proclaiming and criticizing. I think the points on which protest has been demanded of me and given by me are now well enough known. Obviously there may be other such situations in the future. In a world like ours—a world of war, riot, murder, racism, tyranny and established banditry, one has to be able to stand up and say "NO." But there are also other things to do. I am more and more convinced of the reality of my own job which is meditation and study and prayer in silence. I do not intend to give up writing, that too is obviously my vocation. But I hope I will be able to give up controversy some day. Pray for me. When one gets older (Jan. 31 is my fifty-second birthday) one realizes the futility of a life wasted in argument when it should be given entirely to love.

God bless you. I really appreciate your letters. When there are really urgent questions and problems in them, I always do my level best to answer. Please understand that my visits are severely limited and I cannot possibly even think of seeing more than a few people who ask to see me. But there is such a thing as being united in prayer, or even through desire (if you can't pray) and in our friendship. The main thing is that we desire good for each other and seek within the limits of our power to obtain for each other what we desire.

CIRCULAR LETTER TO FRIENDS:
"SEPTUAGESIMA SUNDAY 1967," IN THE ROAD TO JOY

There is no joy but in the victory of Christ over death in us: and all love that is valid has something of that victory. But the power of love cannot "win" in us if we insist on opposing it with something else to which we can cling, on which we trust because we ourselves can manipulate it. It all depends on who is in control: our own ego, or Christ. We must learn to surrender our ego-mastery to His mastery. And this implies a certain independence even of apparently holy systems and routines, official "answers" and infallible gimmicks of every kind. Easter celebrates the victory of love over everything. *Amor vincit omnia.* If we believe it, we still understand it, because belief is what opens the door to love. But to believe only in systems and statements and not in *people* is an evasion, a betrayal of love. When we really believe as Christians, we find ourselves trusting and accepting *people* as well as dogmas. Woe to us when we are merely orthodox, and reject human beings, flesh and blood, the aspirations, joys and needs of men. Yet there is no fruit, either, in merely sentimental gestures of communion that mean little, and seek only to flatter or placate. Love can also be tough and uncompromising in its fidelity to its own highest principles. Let us be united in joy, peace and prayer this Easter and always. "Fear not," says Jesus. "It is I. I am with you all days!"

CIRCULAR LETTER TO FRIENDS:
"EASTER 1967," IN *THE ROAD TO JOY*

*M*y first and last words in this book are, then, to summarize whatever "witness" these pages may contain. When a man enters a monastery he has to stand before the community, and formally responds to a ritual question: *Quid petis?* "What do you ask?" His answer is not that he seeks a happy life, or escape from anxiety, or freedom from sin, or moral perfection, or the summit of contemplation. The answer is that he seeks *mercy.* "The mercy of God and of the Order." Whatever else it may do, this book should bear witness to the fact that I have found what I sought and continue to find it. The Order has been patient with me, God has been merciful to me, and more, countless readers have given me a gift of friendship and love which is to me precious beyond estimation.

These readers sometimes write to me, and generally I am not able to reply. But here at least let me assure them of my gratitude, my love and my prayers. They are in my silence, in my Mass and in my solitude. I hope we will be together in Paradise.

A THOMAS MERTON READER

WORKS BY
THOMAS MERTON
CITED IN THE TEXT

Bread in the Wilderness. New York: New Directions, 1953.

The Collected Poems of Thomas Merton. New York: New Directions, 1977.

Contemplation in a World of Action. New York: Doubleday, 1971.

Contemplative Prayer. New York: Herder and Herder, 1969.

Disputed Questions. New York: Farrar, Straus & Cudahy, 1960.

The Hidden Ground of Love: The Letters of Thomas Merton on Religious Experience and Social Concerns. Edited by William H. Shannon. New York: Farrar, Straus & Giroux, 1985.

Honorable Reader: Reflections on My Work. Edited by Robert E. Daggy. New York: Crossroad, 1989.

The Monastic Journey. Edited by Brother Patrick Hart. Kansas City, MO: Sheed Andrews and McMeel, 1977.

Monastic Life at Gethsemani. Trappist, KY: Abbey of Gethsemani, 1965.

No Man Is an Island. New York: Harcourt, Brace, 1955.

The Road to Joy: Letters to New and Old Friends. Edited by Robert E. Daggy. New York: Farrar, Straus & Giroux, 1989.

The Seven Storey Mountain. New York: Harcourt, Brace, 1948.

Silence in Heaven: A Book on the Monastic Life. New York: Thomas Y. Crowell, 1956.

The Silent Life. New York: Farrar, Straus and Cudahy, 1957.

A Thomas Merton Reader. Edited by Thomas P. McDonnell. New York: Harcourt, Brace & World, Inc., 1962.

Thoughts in Solitude. New York: Farrar, Straus and Cudahy, 1958.

$\mathscr{A}$CKNOWLEDGMENTS

Reprinted by permission of The Crossroad Publishing Company:

Excerpts by Thomas Merton from *Honorable Reader: Reflections on My Work*, edited by Robert E. Daggy. Copyright © 1989 by the Merton Legacy Trust.

Reprinted by permission of Doubleday:

Excerpts from *Contemplation in a World of Action* by Thomas Merton. Copyright © 1969, 1970, 1971, 1973 by the Merton Legacy trust, used by permission of Doubleday, a division of Bantam Doubleday Dell Publishing Group.

Reprinted by permission of Farrar, Straus and Giroux, LLC:

Excerpts from *Disputed Questions* by Thomas Merton. Copyright © 1960 by the Abbey of Our Lady of Gethsemani. Copyright renewed 1988 by Alan Hanson.

Excerpts from *The Hidden Ground of Love: The Letters of Thomas Merton on Religious Experience and Social Concerns* by Thomas Merton, edited by William H. Shannon. Copyright © 1985 by the Merton Legacy Trust.

Excerpts from *The Road to Joy: The Letters of Thomas Merton to New and Old Friends* by Thomas Merton, selected and edited by Robert E. Daggy. Copyright © 1989 by the Merton Legacy Trust.

Excerpts from *The Silent Life* by Thomas Merton. Copyright © 1957 by the Abbey of Our Lady of Gethsemani. Copyright renewed 1985 by the Merton Legacy Trust.

Excerpts from *Thoughts in Solitude* by Thomas Merton. Copyright © 1958 by the Abbey of Our Lady of Gethsemani. Copyright renewed 1986 by the Trustees of the Merton Legacy Trust.

116